THE CHANGING
North Oxford

BOOK ONE

Ann Spokes Symonds

Robert Boyd
PUBLICATIONS

Published by
Robert Boyd Publications
260 Colwell Drive
Witney, Oxfordshire OX8 7LW

First published 1997

ISBN 1 899536 25 6

OTHER TITLES IN THE *CHANGING FACES* SERIES

Banbury: Book One
Bladon with Church Hanborough and Long Hanborough
Botley and North Hinksey
Cowley
Cowley: Book Two
Cumnor and Appleton with Farmoor and Eaton
St Clements and East Oxford: Book One
St Clements and East Oxford: Book Two
Eynsham: Book One
Headington: Book One
Headington: Book Two
Jericho: Book One
Littlemore and Sandford
Marston: Book One
Marston: Book Two
Summertown and Cutteslowe
St Ebbes and St Thomas: Book One
St Ebbes and St Thomas: Book Two
Wolvercote with Wytham and Godstow
Woodstock: Book One
Woodstock: Book Two

FORTHCOMING

Bicester: Book One
Cowley: Book Three
Cowley Works
Eynsham: Book Two
Faringdon and District
Jericho: Book Two
North Oxford: Book Two
Oxford City Centre: Book One
South Oxford
Thame
Witney: Book One
West Oxford

Printed and bound by the Alden Group, Oxford and Northampton

Contents

Cover illustrations

Front: Some of the staff and pupils at Wychwood, Miss Batty's School, 1911.
(Part of a photograph which appears in full on page 43.)

Back: Map of Norham Manor and vicinity.

Acknowledgements

Having spent my childhood and undergraduate years living in North Oxford, I have particularly enjoyed working on this book. I have been able to meet old friends and make new ones and I am indebted to all those who have kindly lent me photographs. These have been individually acknowledged in the text. However, I should like to thank others who have helped me, including Mr Jeremy Baraquin, Mrs Mary Blaschko, Mrs Sara Briggs, Ms Julie Courtenay, Mr John Cole, Mr Jeremy Daniel, Mr Peter Davey, Mr Bill Dickins and Mr Philip Platt of the Oxfordshire Museums Store, Mrs Escritt, Dr Malcom Graham of the Centre for Oxfordshire Studies, Mr Hale of Wolfson College, Mrs Catriona Jones, Mr David Jowett, Mrs Rosemary Morgan, Dr Desmond Morris, Dr Katherine Peet, Miss Deborah Quare, Dr Marjorie Reeves, the Reverend Max Saint, Mrs Herta Babette Simon, Mr Graham Simpson, Ms Jane Smith, Mrs Peggy Smith, Ms Jackie Wallace-Jones, Mrs Clare Wenham, Miss Phyllis White and Mrs Eileen Wright.

I should also like to thank my husband Richard Symonds for all his help and encouragement, Dr Desmond Walshaw for his indispensable computer skills and Mr Fred Toon of Central Systems for his experience and patience in laser-copying many of the photographs.

Every effort has been made to trace the copyright owners of two photographs and two drawings without success and anyone claiming copyright should please get in touch with me.

Ann Spokes Symonds

Introduction

North Oxford is so rich in buildings, people, educational establishments and social history that this book, the first in the series about this area of Oxford, is confined to Norham Manor. Walton Manor will be the subject of Book Two.

A map showing the roads which are covered by this book can be found on the back cover. Woodstock Road south of Lathbury Road and the area to the west of it, stretching as far as Walton Street, will be included in Book Two.

NOTE ON THE PHOTOGRAPHS

Some of the original photographs were faded or unsharp and did not reproduce well but I have included a few for historical reasons or to illustrate a point. I hope that readers will therefore forgive the quality in order that they can at least gain some impression and be able to appreciate the atmosphere of the place, group or event.

Buildings and Gardens

There was open country between St Giles and the small settlements of Wolvercote and Summertown before North Oxford was developed in the 19th century. Exceptions were a few scattered houses in the vicinity of North Parade and some clustered around the Royal Oak Inn in Woodstock Road. In the 1860s strolling along the Banbury road was like taking a country walk although in those days it was not so-called but was known as St Giles' East.

Back in the 14th and 15th centuries the whole of the North Oxford area was called Walton Field. Between 1400 and 1757 there was a gallows for executions on the site of Greenditch, now St Margaret's Road.

St Giles' Church in 1834. On the right are old houses, now a historic hotel by the name of the Old Parsonage which is 17th century (listed Grade II of special architectural or historic interest). It is on the site of Bethlem, a haven for poor people. The animals in the fore-ground are probably being driven to market. (See also Churches.)

The Old Parsonage as it is today.

It is often supposed that the development of North Oxford began when dons were allowed to marry but in fact the celibacy rule was not abolished until the 1870s and before then wealthy traders and others inhabited houses which had been built for them. Once the dons could marry they were still required to live within 1½ miles of Carfax.

Park Town was the first to be developed. It was known as St Giles Field until 1849 and was then the property of New College. Two architects submitted their drawings for it in 1853, E.G. Bruton and S.L. Seckham of which the latter was chosen. Until this date there had been other plans for the area, including a workhouse (when Park Town was owned by the Guardians of the Poor) and even a railway line with subsidiary buildings. In 1858 it was the property of the Park Town Estate Company.

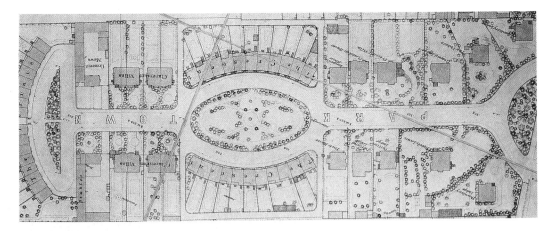

Seckham's plan and lay-out of Park Town (courtesy of Park Town Trustees). The detached Italianate villas are nearest the Banbury Road, then (eastwards) the Crescent, then the semi-detached 'Clarendon Villas' with mews and stables and finally the Terrace. There is an attractive central garden with many mature trees. The small half-circle on the Banbury Road was the site of a public convenience from 1926 to 1996. There is now only a small, enclosed electricity sub-station there and replanting has taken place.

Although Park Town was not at first a financial success, the houses were occupied by the beginning of the 1860s. All of Park Town has been listed as being of special architectural or historic interest (Grade II) since 1972. In the 1930s, it became a haven for some exiled intellectuals.

Opposite. Photographs taken in 1997, clockwise from top left. The north side of the Crescent. A statue in the central garden. The central garden. The railings which were replaced by the Friends of Park Town (in place of the original cast-iron ones which were taken away in the Second World War) are being painted. The archway of the Terrace looking through to Dragon (Lynam's) Lane. The Terrace from the north-west. Herta Babette Simon, Park Town historian, outside her home, 37 Park Town. Note the recently restored railings which are a true copy of the original wrought-iron patterns on hand-rails. One of the Clarendon Villas. Centre: Listed Victorian 'Hexagonal Penfold' type letter-box and recent notice board.

Park Town has, through the years, escaped the criticisms levelled at the Victorian Gothic architecture of Norham Manor which, throughout its history, has been admired and ridiculed, romanticised and threatened. In the 1960s, much of Norham Manor was on the point of being annihilated and replaced by extensions to the Science Area and other University buildings. Architects of the day, like Lionel Brett, could not wait to design their own buildings to take the place of the Victorian Gothic for which they had no liking.

It was only by the skin of their teeth that the houses were saved from demolition and became a Conservation Area. Sir John Betjeman, often called the Bard of North Oxford, agreed to contact the right people, thus helping to save the houses for posterity. He had always been a lover of North Oxford, describing the houses as 'each learning something from Christ Church Cathedral and the Parks Museum. Each house repeats it in its own special way. Ever-changing, never the same.'

62 Banbury Road, originally known as 'Ketilby' (taken in 1965 by P.S. Spokes). It was built in 1865 for the Reverend St J Tyrwhitt, Vicar of St Mary Magdalen from 1858 to 1872, and the architect was E.G. Bruton. Tyrwhitt was an amateur artist and patron of the arts who had worked with William Morris and John Hungerford Pollen at the Oxford Union where he painted the ceiling. The house is now the home of University departments. It is listed Grade II.

The Ruskinian carving over the doorway of No. 62 (taken in 1997) is by J.H. Pollen (1820–1902) and illustrates some lines in Proverbs:

A lion which is strongest among beasts and a greyhound and a goat and *a king against whom there is no rising up.*

Number 60 Banbury Road (originally called 'Shrublands'). The drawing comes from the book *English Country Houses* (1875) by the architect W. Wilkinson. Built in 1869, like No. 62 it is listed (Grade II).

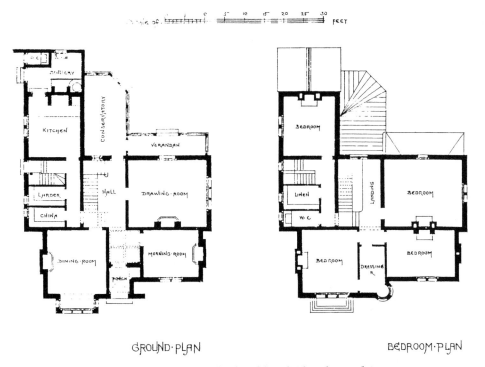

GROUND·PLAN   BEDROOM·PLAN

Ground floor plan of 'Shrublands' by the architect.

'Shrublands' in 1965 (P.S.Spokes). The house was first leased to T.G. Cousins (chemist). It is now occupied by the Pitt Rivers Museum and others. Both 60 and 62 were threatened with demolition in the early 1960s to make way for a new Pitt Rivers Museum.

Part of a letter written by Sir John Betjeman with inset photograph of him (courtesy of Margaret Bonfiglioli). The letter was written in 1962 in reply to one from a local City Councillor in which he writes: 'With the slow invasion of the drearier parts of the University into North Oxford, the salvation of the Norham Estate at any rate is important.' As a first step he wrote to the Royal Fine Art Commission enclosing the Councillor's letter in which she had pleaded for the official scheduling of the best Victorian buildings in North Oxford so that they could be saved from demolition. At that time there were no Conservation Areas.

St John's College had bought what was to become the Norham Gardens Estate in 1573 from Richard Owen (son of the physician to Henry VIII) for £1566. However, the first wave of development did not begin until 1833. The artist Holman Hunt said that by about 1850 the University taste for modern Gothic was established beyond recall. St John's commissioned the Oxfordshire architect William Wilkinson (1819–1901) to lay out the estate and most of the houses were designed by him and by Frederick Codd, E.G. Bruton, Charles Buckeridge and John Gibbs.

The college, who let the houses on 99-year leases, laid down rules about density and it was they who insisted that the front gardens should have low walls and iron railings so that they could be seen. One of the most attractive features of North Oxford is the subtle curves of the roads seen, for instance, in Bradmore, Winchester and Staverton Roads.

Norham Road from the corner of Fyfield Road (1997). Note the low walls in front. St John's also insisted that the mature trees should be preserved and, in fact, expected every lease-holder to apply for permission even to lop a tree. Mrs Osler, wife of the great physician William Osler, complained that 'it needed an Act of Parliament to allow sunlight to our windows'.

Another example of leafy North Oxford (1997), showing a mature tree on the corner of Charlbury and Bardwell Roads.

North Oxford also has the advantage of conifers and non-deciduous trees so that it keeps its verdant look even in winter. Christina Colvin remembers all the houses in Norham Gardens in the 1920s having clipped bushes behind diamond-patterned railings with gates to match. Popular flowering trees were (and still are) laburnum, pink and red may, almond and sometimes cherry. Ivy or Virginia creeper covered the brickwork, climbing right to the top.

Betjeman sums up the beauty of North Oxford in *Summoned by Bells*:

> *'Take me centaur-bike down Linton Road*
> *Gliding by newly-planted almond trees,*
> *Show me thy road, Crick, in the early Spring,*
> *Laurel and privet and laburnum ropes.*

Favourite garden plants were lauristinos, mahonias, hollies, berberis, pampas grass and yuccas. Typical was the rope-shaped brick edging to the beds, still to be seen in some gardens. In the early days island beds in the lawns were popular, semi-circular or kidney-shaped, edged with low box with a weeping tree in the centre.

One of William Wilkinson's designs for a house and garden. This was the home of the Oslers (see Families) from 1906. Note the island flower bed in the foreground and the croquet lawn. A different conservatory was built for the house, 13 Norham Gardens, when it was erected in 1869 for its original owner, Thomas Dallin, tutor at The Queen's College. The Oslers added on to the house, as did many owners, not only to house larger families but to add a conservatory or indoor fernery.

An example of houses built in 1889 in Rawlinson Road which is one of the few roads not to take its name from a St John's living. It was named after Dr Richard Rawlinson, the 18th century divine. These (from left to right) are Nos. 8, 6 and 4. The architect of both No. 6 and No. 8 was H. Quinton.

Number 6 Rawlinson Road from its front gate. Many of the houses in this road are still in family use.

It is the gardens, trees and flowering shrubs of North Oxford which have delighted the eye for generations whatever people have thought about the architecture. Pevsner describes it as having an air of 'leafy sobriety'. Thomas Sharp, the planner, who was no lover of Gothic buildings, thought that the only reason for saving North Oxford was its beautiful trees. Others have been more critical of the Gothic villas over the years. One of the first was the Reverend W. Tuckwell in *Oxford Reminiscences* (1900) who described the 'interminable streets of villadom.'

During the first half of the 20th century, the architecture had few friends. Penelope Lively, prize-winning author and Oxford graduate, in her novel *The House in Norham Gardens* (1974), described the houses as having 'tottered over the edge into madness.'

'These are not houses,' she writes, 'but flights of fancy. They are three storeys high and disguise themselves as churches. They have ecclesiastical porches instead of front doors ... they have nineteen rooms and half a dozen chimneys and iron fire escapes. You had to be a fat busy Victorian family to expand enough to fill up basements and conservatories and attics. You had to have bootboys and nurses and parlourmaids.'

By the late 1960s, the majority of the larger houses, built for large families with domestic staff, had been converted into flats, student accommodation or adapted for institutional use.

An example of a converted house. 'Gunfield', 19 Norham Gardens (Frederick Codd), 1877, was for many years the home of the Misses Deneke in whose music room played such great names as Casals, Myra Hess, Gervase Elwes, Schweitzer and Sir Donald Tovey. The house has recently been restored and converted to student accommodation by St Edmund Hall and has been awarded a plaque by the Oxford Preservation Trust for its careful restoration and discreet improvements.

Bradmore Road houses from the west. On the left are the semi-detached Nos. 10 (left) and 9. To the right is No. 8. Numbers 9 and 10 were at one time a Radcliffe Infirmary Nurses' Home but are now the annexe to Green College. Numbers 5–8 are owned by Linacre College. This was the road in which in earlier times lived Walter Pater, who had such an influence on North Oxford life, Sir Halford MacKinder (founder of modern geography), Professor Sir Ray Lankaster and Mrs Humphrey Ward. (Photograph taken from Wolsey Hall, 1997, kindness of Oxford English Centre.)

Number 14 Norham Gardens, the home of Mr and Mrs Arthur Gray Butler (see Families) from 1887. Designed by Codd, the first leaseholder was the Hon W.E. Sackville-West, Bursar of Keble, for whom Codd added a wing in 1874 to provide a large dining-room to cope with the dinner parties. In the 1960s it was the home of Oxfordshire County Library. Both numbers 14 and 16, joined by a modern addition, are owned by the Cherwell Centre Ltd. (Taken in 1997.)

In the 1960s it was thought that if the houses were not demolished they would be impracticable for family use. Peter Howell, of the Victorian Group, contradicted this and 'could only say, as those fortunate to live in them can attest, that it is simply not true. They are,' he said, 'for the most part astonishingly adaptable.'

The unadaptability of North Oxford villas may have been a myth put about by members of the University who were opposed to the Conservation Area and who would have preferred land to be zoned for University use. The Victorian Group of the Oxford Architectural and Historical Society was set up in 1966 with Mrs Catherine Cole, who lived in Norham Road and was also the energetic Secretary of the OAHS, as the prime instigator. She brought together an enthusiastic group of supporters who met regularly at her home and worked hard to preserve all those houses not already lost and to make sure that alterations were sympathetically undertaken. Another of their causes concerned opposition to the erosion of front gardens by tarmac. Mr John Ashdown has for many years also been a friend of North Oxford in his capacity as the City Council's Conservation Officer.

Number 18 Norham Gardens (built in 1872) is yet another conversion but in this case to flats. The original architect was Frederick Codd. Note that, despite the loss of some garden to gravel and parked cars, the retention of the shrubs and small trees and the iron railings help it to retain its character. It was first inhabited by the Reverend Professor Palmer and more recently by the Bonfiglioli family where Margaret Bonfiglioli followed in her mother's profession (see Slater Family) and had a long stream of lodgers many of whom became distinguished writers, archaeologists and artists. The attic room at the top of the right gable was the most popular room. Her husband Kyril was an art dealer.

Number 121 Banbury Road (front) in the mid-1920s. The home of Mr and Mrs Frederick Swinson (he is seen in the foreground). Not a St John's house, it was built in the Edwardian style, so different from Norham Gardens.

Number 121 Banbury Road from the back with the gardener in the centre. It later became a hostel for and then the main home of the nuns of Springfield St Mary who added an attractive chapel. Today it is part of St Clare's and seems to have adapted well to institutional use.

'Fairfield', 115 Banbury Road (taken in 1997 from the back). Another Edwardian-style house with attractive gardens which has for 50 years been in institutional use. Now a private residential home, it has some sensitively designed modern additions to the north and south of the original house. It opened with just eight residents in 1947, the first secretary and virtual founder being Mrs Clare Kreyer. It was formerly the home of the Legge family where the two Misses Legge returned to live (in the 1970s) to join many other elderly ladies of North Oxford who have found comfort and friendship there. Their father, James Legge, was the first Professor of Chinese at Oxford.

On the Bardwell Estate (its original name), which ran northwards to Belbroughton Road, the front gardens have unpretentious wooden, slatted fencing about a metre high with only a few layers of brick beneath, which allows the flowering shrubs to be seen from the road. Long stretches of the original fencing, erected between 70 and 100 years ago, remain, giving the whole area a restful, restrained continuity.

Fencing at 26 Charlbury Road in 1924, a year after the house was built.

The same house in 1997.

Houses in the new (1980s) north-east extension to Charlbury Road where low walls have replaced fencing (taken in 1997).

'Belbroughton Road is bonny, and pinkly bursts the spray
Of prunus and forsythia across the public way.'

John Betjeman

Belbroughton Road in the winter of 1930–31, looking east (courtesy of Helen Lock). Howard Colvin, the architectural historian in his book *Unbuilt Oxford,* says that only in Belbroughton Road will the connoiseur of neo-Georgian find a small group of houses worth his attention. They were built between 1925 and 1938.

Number 1 Belbroughton Road taken in 1997. Built in 1926, the architect was Christopher Wright who was responsible for six other houses in the road, Nos. 1–5 Garford Road and Nos. 28, 32 and 34 Charlbury Road.

Belbroughton Road in 1977 at the time of the Queen's Jubilee celebrations. The street party, organised by Mrs Yvonne Hands, was attended by local residents. Included in the pictures are Lady Simon (see Families), Nesta Selwyn, Geoffrey Dawes, Sir David Yardley and the local bobby on his bicycle. (Courtesy Lady Yardley.)

Hotels

Mention has already been made of the Old Parsonage at 3 Banbury Road, one of the oldest establishments in North Oxford. There both Oscar Wilde and Compton Mackenzie stayed as undergraduates. Though much restored, it has some original fireplaces and early 18th century panelling.

Linton Lodge Hotel, prestigious and peaceful. It started in a small way in the house on the corner of Linton and Charlbury Roads owned by Mr A. Retey, a master at the Dragon school. He realised that there was a need for somewhere for Dragon parents to stay when visiting their offspring. It gradually expanded, taking over the large house of the Whitley family when they moved from Oxford. (Taken in 1997.)

A wedding reception in the garden of Linton Lodge in the 1950s, a popular place for North Oxford people to celebrate. (Courtesy Heather Retey.)

Patrick (later Sir Patrick) Nairne and Penelope (Penny) Bridges leaving for their honeymoon after their wedding reception at Linton Lodge in September 1948. The Bridges family lived at 24 Charlbury Road.

The Cotswold Lodge Hotel on the corner of Banbury and Norham Roads, another popular and well-patronised establishment. A typical North Oxford villa, designed by Wilkinson and built in 1863, it has been extended by modern additions in keeping with the original building. (Taken in 1997.) For Parklands Hotel, see Families.

Drawing the Line

In its early days North Oxford was a close-knit community of mainly University people who were anxious to keep it as their own preserve. Although wealthy traders and some professional people not connected with academic life lived side by side with the professors and dons there was much snobbery, and town and gown rarely mixed socially. In 1826, for instance, T. Little in *Confessions of an Oxonian* went so far as to suggest that 'pastry cooks who had made fortunes out of cheating members of the University should not pollute the magnificent entrances to the most beautiful of cities in the kingdom.'

Max Müller, who came to Oxford from Germany in 1848, remarked on the fact that City Society was completely separated from University Society, so that even rich bankers and other gentlemen would never have ventured to ask members of the University to dine.

The Mount, Banbury Road, the home of G.P. Hester, Town Clerk and solicitor, in 1914. Successful tradesmen and businessmen had been some of the first to inhabit the big villas in North Oxford. Hester had leased land from University College to build The Mount and its lodge. People dubbed his house 'Quillville'. The house of Thomas Mallam, once a tobacconist but later an auctioneer and Mayor of Oxford, was popularly known as 'Quidville' and an ironmonger's house was 'Tinville'. Hester died in 1876. The Mount was pulled down in the First World War and was replaced by buildings for St Hugh's College. (Copyright Bodleian Library, Oxford, Ref. Minn 6/1.)

Mrs A.L. Smith (whose husband became Master of Balliol) lived in Crick Road when they first came to Oxford and she admits, in her biography of her husband, that Oxford Society in 1878—79 was a 'very small world indeed' and beyond that Society no one, so to speak, counted. One dignified lady of that time told her that once there had been only four University ladies — 'a delightful circle' — whereas by 1878 there were 20 and steadily increasing.

Snobbery was rife. One elderly lady who had, as she presumed, achieved greatness by marrying a Fellow of Brasenose College and who had been living in North Oxfordshire, returned as a widow to live in Beaumont Street. When the wife of a leading surgeon called on this widow she got an icy reception and was told that she must not expect her visit to be returned as 'the line must be drawn somewhere'.

In 1857 when Charles Mostyn Owen came back to Oxford and lived at Walton House (later part of Somerville), he was Chief Constable of Oxfordshire Police. Though warmly welcomed by County Society and he had come up from Rugby to Trinity (in 1837) and was an Oxford M.A., he was not welcomed by University Society and their reception was 'distinctly chilly'. His daughter, in her memoirs, recalls that 'credentials which were a good enough passport to County Society were not valid in the University'. 'I think', she wrote, 'my parents were more surprised and amused than annoyed to find themselves treated as outsiders.' In the 19th century, if the next door neighbour was a tradesman a don's children would never know them. The University, professional people, clergy and distant relatives of the aristocracy were considered upper middle class and the successful traders lower middle class.

MIDDLE CLASS DAY SCHOOL FOR GIRLS.

WINCHESTER ROAD, OXFORD.

Established in 1858.

CONDUCTED BY

Sisters of the

Society of the Holy and Undivided Trinity,

of The Convent, Oxford.

VISITOR THE LORD BISHOP OF OXFORD.

Hours of School.

Morning 9. 15. to 12. 30.   Afternoon 2. to 4. 15.

The School Terms begin January 1st. May 1st, September 1st.

The School Fee, eleven shillings per Term, to be paid in advance.

COURSE OF INSTRUCTION.

English, French, Drawing, Class Singing, Drill and Needlework.

EXTRA.

Instrumental Music. Copy, exercise, and home lesson books.

The School is under Government and Diocesan Inspection.

Children received from three years old.

The School is recommended by the :—

REV. C. DAVEY BIGGS, D. D. the REV. the RURAL DEAN. the REV. W. B. DUGGAN and MISS BULL, Arncott House. Application to be made to the MOTHER SUPERIOR, the Convent, or to the HEAD MISTRESS, at the School House.

This school even advertised itself for the middle classes. This was for the children of college servants and small tradesmen. St John's College at first opposed the school, considering it would mean a deterioration in the value of the land.

When the new Girls' High School was begun in 1875 at 16 St Giles, it meant that social class divisions had to be dismantled. Not only had the daughters of the professional classes to sit and play with tradesmen's children but different University and political feelings had to be suppressed. There had even been a pro-German social group and a pro-French group.

Even as late as 1925 there were some strange snobbish views held about the High School. When a don's wife heard that the Warden of New College and his wife intended to send their daughter Mary there (she later became Principal of St Hilda's College) she asked if they were not afraid that she would 'pick up an accent.'

By the beginning of the 20th century, North Oxford became less socially isolated and many non-academic people moved there as a pleasant place to live. Retired Indian and Colonial servants (some with knighthoods) and army officers bought houses in the area and mixed easily with the dons' families. In the 1930s onwards people distinguished in other fields came and played an active part in the community such as Air-Vice Marshall MacNeece Foster (Lord Mayor of Oxford) who lived at 23 Linton Road and Major-General Sir Robert McCarrison (Churchwarden of St Andrew's) who lived at 18 Northmoor Road.

Air-Vice Marshal MacNeece Foster and his wife when Lord Mayor and Lady Mayoress in June 1966.

Even in recent years, North Oxford has retained a flavour of its own. Peter Snow, in his perceptive book *Oxford Observed* (1991) listed numerous special characteristics of North Oxford people including 'taking power is vulgar but influence quite another matter' and 'flaunting wealth is the greatest sin and a recipe for social disaster'. There is competition especially concerning children's progress at school, 'how many people you can attract to your dinner table and how well your last book did.' 'But mainly', Snow writes, 'the rivalry is to do with how closely in cuisine, clothes and life-style you can approximate to the right North Oxford note of understated quality and good taste.' Despite the houses being split up for multi-occupation there is still a large population of academics. In 1990, for instance, the electoral role of St Andrew's Church had 20 PhD's on it.

Drawing the line round North Oxford itself is not easy. Usually it is considered to run from north of St Giles in the south to Belbroughton Road and Lathbury Roads in the north. Beyond this is Summertown. In the west it includes Woodstock Road and the side roads which run westwards to Walton Street and Hayfield Road. In the east is included the University Parks.

Once, a librarian, newly appointed to a post in Oxford in the 1970s, was telling his new colleagues that he lived in North Oxford when he was overheard by his new boss's secretary. Afterwards she came up to him saying: 'Excuse me but I must point out that you don't live in North Oxford.' It took him a while to understand that Linkside Avenue, where he had come to live, was not in North Oxford. He was puzzled where it could be because, to him, newly arrived, it was definitely North.

Visiting and Visiting Cards

Visiting was very much part of North Oxford life and continued at least until the time of the Second World War. There were certain rules which had to be followed concerning the visiting cards which, once received, were usually kept on a plate or silver tray in people's halls or hallways, resting on a table near the door. If the corner of the card was turned down it meant that the owner had delivered it in person. Otherwise, it had been brought by someone else on their behalf.

A selection of visiting cards (courtesy of Mrs Margaret Pinsent). Note that men's cards usually bore their college address but cards bearing the names of ladies (unless their home was in college like the Poyntons or Lady Salter) included their home address.

Mrs Butcher, who lived in Bradmore Road in the 1890s, insisted that top-hats be worn by gentlemen when they made Sunday calls. Mrs A.L. Smith (see Families) remembers a pyramid of cards piled up in her drawing-room in the early 1880s. She also read in *The Queen,* which also then bore the additional title *The Lady's Newspaper,* in the 1890s, that visiting cards were never sent by post. If that had been possible she thought she might have left Crick Road, where they lived at one time, without a stain on her character. She did not have time to visit much and this had been noticed. Once she had a bit of a conscience about her bad record and made six calls on one day. An old friend, Mrs Vernon Harcourt, consequently rushed round the next day to enquire whether anything was wrong. Mrs Smith's daughter, Barbara (Lady Cairns), seemed to have inherited this trait as she also let the visiting cards pile up and they were discovered years later with such names as Lady Trevelyan on them.

In Victorian times many ladies had an 'At Home' every week when visitors called and were served tea. The invitation cards of Mrs Hatch carried the words 'Tea' and '4–6 pm'. She sent one to Lewis Carroll who was a friend of the family and an admirer of her little girls, but he refused, writing: 'What an awful proposition. To drink tea from 4 to 6 would tax the constitution even of a hardened tea drinker.' He preferred to visit on his own as the only guest. Walter Pater, however, was happy to visit the Hatchs. He always wore a peacock-blue tie through a ring.

Mrs Haldane, (see Families), wife of Profesor J.S. Haldane, wrote in her book *Friends and Kindred* that a few months after their wedding in 1891, Lady Burdon-Sanderson, wife of the Regius Professor of Medicine, Mrs Haldane's aunt and sister of the then Lord Chancellor, asked all the right people to call on her but thought University society very limited. Mrs Haldane recounts a queer happening. Her parlour-maid 'hid in a back drawer on the hall table the cards of several people I should have liked to know' she wrote. 'I found them over a year later and heard from the other servant that the parlour-maid had told her that she would not show them to me as I had far more visitors than was good for me.'

Silver trays and cards.

One day soon after their arrival in Garford Road in the 1920s, Mrs Ena Galbraith (see Families) took her children to school as usual (Jane to the High School and Jim to the Dragon) after which she did some shopping and had lunch before returning home in the afternoon. She was surprised to find a woman she did not know sitting in her drawing-room. The room was the smaller of the two living rooms as her husband, a newly appointed don at Balliol, had the larger one for his books and study. The lady sat there demurely in hat and gloves. Mrs Galbraith had no time to take off her own hat or get tidy before the door opened and another lady in hat and gloves appeared. In the end about 20–25 women came, squeezed into the room, and stayed for some time chatting. Herring, the Galbraith's cook-housekeeper, who had been a Barnardo's boy and was not used to gracious living, brought in the tea. The mystery was solved later when it was explained to Mrs Galbraith that it was the tradition for dons' wives to call on newcomers on the first Monday of the academic term. No one had thought to tell her.

If you went to tea with a don's wife it was she who was in charge. Wives took the status of their husbands. Mrs Galbraith, for instance, despite having a PhD from Manchester, was just the wife of a junior don at Balliol. Lady Cairns (see Families), daughter of the Master of Balliol and a Cambridge graduate, liked to make a statement about her status by wearing an apron in the house.

When the Simons (see Families) came to Oxford from Germany in 1933 they bought a house in Belbroughton Road. On the day they moved in, Mrs Charlotte (later Lady) Simon was telling the removal men where to put their large pieces of furniture which they had been permitted to bring from their German home. A lady had already come to call and was calmly sitting in the drawing-room. It was after the third request from a remover: 'Where shall we put this?', that her guest decided to go, suggesting that another time might be more convenient. She placed her visiting card on the mantlepiece and later when Charlotte looked at it, she saw that it bore the name of Lady Mary Murray. Both Gilbert and Lady Mary, stalwart champions of refugees and the oppressed, had been responsible for persuading ICI to give scientific fellowships which enabled German refugees like Simon to take up posts in Oxford. Her early call of welcome was therefore understandable.

Colleges, Schools and Institutions

Colleges

Lady Margaret Hall (LMH)

Four of the women's colleges are in North Oxford and two of them, Lady Margaret Hall and St Hugh's, come into the area of this book on Norham Manor. It was because of the energy and enthusiasm of so many wives of academics that further education in Oxford began. As early as 1866 a few North Oxford women had obtained permission to attend University lectures given by relatives and friends. From 1870 Ruskin, Slade Professor of Fine Art, whose lectures were always popular, particularly invited women to attend. Young North Oxford women were keen to improve their minds and looked forward to the days when there would be colleges for women.

In 1873, a group of women, including Bertha Johnson, who was to become the first Principal of the Society of Home Students (later St Anne's College), Louise Creighton, Georgina Max Müller (see Families), Charlotte Green, Mary (Mrs Humphrey) Ward, Clara Pater and Lavinia Talbot, whose husbands or brothers were Professors or dons, started up a series of lectures which were well attended by North Oxford women. Husbands of these ladies were some of the first to give encouragement and backing to the starting up of women's halls of residence which later became colleges. Notable supporters also included Mark Pattison, Arthur Sidgwick, Sir Henry Acland and H.A.L. Fisher.

The Association for the Education of Women was set up in 1878 and the foundation of Lady Margaret Hall happened soon afterwards, being established as a Church of England institution. Somerville (non-denominational) and St Anne's (then the Society of Home Students) followed in 1879. St Hugh's was founded in 1886. Annie Rogers, a great pioneer of women's education, thought the reason the earlier women's colleges succeeded was that they were in North Oxford. It was not until 1920, however, that women were able to take degrees. Now, all four women's colleges in North Oxford are co-residential.

A group of women students at Lady Margaret Hall in 1886. Back row, left to right: H.M. Mitchell, R.M. Woodhouse, S.F. Carr, M.C. Crowder, J.E. Hogarth, B.M. Layman, C.M. Rivington, M. Benson, B.M. Berkley, E. Langridge, O.M.D. Shroder, M.F. Meredith. Middle row: G.E. Mitchell, E.M.C. Sharp, A. Holmes, E.F. Jourdain, Miss Wordsworth, (Principal), C. Pownall, E.M. Argles, K.P. Hammond. Front row: T. Prestidge, M. Dormer-Harris, H.M. Woodhead, S.M. Taylor, G.M.L. Bell, E.E. Fletcher. (Courtesy of Lady Margaret Hall).

LMH hockey XI in 1916. (Courtesy of Jane Barbour.)

LMH women at a tea party in 1917. In those days they were called 'undergraduettes'. (Courtesy of Jane Barbour.)

Queen Mary in 1921 at the main door of LMH with (far left) her daughter Princess Mary (Princess Royal), the Vice-Chancellor, Dr Farnell, Miss Jex-Blake (Principal) and Miss Lodge, one of the dons.

Afterwards the Principal showed the Queen round the buildings where she met the domestic staff and the college cat. Two senior students escorted Princess Mary to the river and boathouse which she was especially keen to see.

On a much later occasion the present Queen opened the new library of LMH.

The Chapel of LMH in the 1930s. It is now enclosed in the college precincts but can be seen from Benson Place.

The front quad of LMH in 1997. Until the new lodge was built this was the main entrance to the college at the northern-most end of Norham Gardens. The architect was Sir Reginald Blomfield.

The new Wolfson building designed by Raymond Erith (1904–1973). This is now the main entrance to the college. It was built in 1959–60. (Taken in 1997.)

St Hugh's College

The first students of St Hugh's College in 1887. Back row, left to right: Jessie Emmerson, Charlotte Jourdain, W. de L. Mitchell. Front row: Miss Moberly, the first Principal, Constance Ashburner, Grace Parsons.

The College was founded in 1886 as a society for women students by Elizabeth Wordsworth, first Principal of LMH (see above) and a great niece of the poet. The College buildings were started in 1916, designed by Buckland and Hayward. There were extensions in 1928, 1936, 1964 and in the 1980s and 1990s. The Principal's Lodgings are now in 'The Shubbery', 72 Woodstock Road.

Starting with four pupils in a rented house at 25 Norham Gardens (and later No 17) it was for girls from modest homes and it was intended to have a 'less luxurious' way of life than at LMH.

St Hugh's in 1890. The Principal, Miss Moberly, is seated in the middle row, second from left, and Miss Wordsworth, who still took a great interest in St Hugh's, is second from right.

The staff at St Hugh's in 1919. Back row, left to right: Miss Spearing, Miss Shaw, Miss Bullen (Bursar), Miss Hind. Front row: Miss Ady, Miss Annie Rogers, Miss Jourdain (Principal), Miss Wardale, Miss Evans. (All above three photographs, courtesy St. Hugh's College).

St Hugh's from the garden (1997).

The memorial sundial (seen in distance, above) to Annie Rogers who was the creator of the well-known garden at the College.

Annie Rogers was a scholar who won an Exhibition at Worcester College at the age of 17 but when they found out that her initials (A.M.A.H.) stood for Annie Mary Anne Henley, and thus she was female, they would not allow her to enter. Her father, Professor Thorold Rogers M.P., was a close friend of Lewis Carroll and when she was a child Carroll photographed her and told her stories. She was a distinguished classicist at St Hugh's. She was a skilled and knowledgeable gardener and collected cuttings from other enthusiasts with their agreement. However, the College porters at St John's were warned that if Miss Rogers was seen in the garden there with an umbrella, where she stored her cuttings, she was not to be allowed to be there on her own. When gardening she wore a man's trilby hat and in cold weather four coats, each shorter than the one underneath. Known as 'The Rodge', she was often seen riding her bicycle, wearing thick boots and heavy woollen stockings and often with complete disregard for the rules of the road. She was killed on her bicycle while crossing St. Giles on a dark, rainy night in 1937.

Wolfson College

The topping-out ceremony at the college on 15th December, 1972. Sir Isaiah Berlin, C.B.E., F.B.A, its first President and in effect the Founder, is seen with trowel together with (left to right) Mr Powell of the Architects Powell and Moya, a representative of the building group, Shepherd of Cambridge, ?, Michael Brock, Vice-President of Wolfson and Warden of Nuffield College 1977–1988. (Photograph courtesy of Wolfson College.) Sir Isaiah (1909–1997) was one of the most

original and influential people in the intellectual life of the country.

The college was first established by the University in 1964 as Iffley College for graduates, originally based at Court Place, Iffley. However, when the larger site of 'Cherwell' (see Haldane Family) became available it was allocated to the Fellows of the college in 1966. A major building grant came from the Wolfson Foundation, hence the name.

Wolfson College B Block in its water-side setting (July 1997). The buildings were opened in 1974. Note the way that the structure curves. The original plan was for straight blocks but Sir Isaiah Berlin had been impressed with the curved buildings he had seen in Portofino, Italy when he was on holiday and he suggested the idea to the architects. A few Fellows called it, informally, 'the Berlin wall.' The River Cherwell is behind the trees in the background. By 1987 the college had over 800 members, all graduate students.

Wolfson College. The block on the north side which complements B Block to the south. (July 1997.)

Schools

The Dragon School

A performance of Gilbert and Sullivan's *Pirates of Penzance* in 1933. All but three of the female parts were played by boys.

The school was started by a group of Oxford graduates, including seven professors and a few heads of colleges, and teaching first took place in Balliol Hall in St Giles in 1877. The school spent some years at 17 Crick Road but moved to its present site in Bardwell Road in 1895. The boys themselves invented the name and it was used from the early days even though the official name, under the Reverend A.E. Clarke, was the Oxford Preparatory School. C.C. Lynam ('Skipper' as he preferrred to be called) succeeded Clarke in 1886 and the school was then informally known as 'Lynam's'. The Dragon name became official in 1921.

A diving competition at the Dragon School in the 1930s. The river has always been an integral and important part of school life. Every child was expected to 'swim the river', across and back, fully clothed. The barge in this photograph, erected as a memorial to Old Dragons and contributed to by parents and pupils, has since been pulled down. The diving board has also gone. Mr Parnell ('the Colonel') is seen seated in swimming suit on the boarded edge between the long diving boards. He taught generations of boys and girls to swim, at first holding them up with stick and rope, like a fishing rod. (Courtesy Dragon School). Seventy-five Old Dragons were killed in the First World War and there is a permanent stone memorial in the grounds.

Dragon families were able to swim there during the summer holidays. This group was taken in August 1937. Left to right: John Spokes, ?, Ann Spokes, ?, ?, ?, Michael (Micky) Jones, ?, Reggie Lodge (lying down), Lilla Spokes, ?.

The 1st XV Rugger team at the Dragon School in 1970. Rugger is played from an early age, even by 'the babies.' Sometimes if it becomes too rough and someone is hurt and starts crying, the others clap with encouragement.
Back row, left to right: A. Chadwick, K. Donovan, J. Phipps, D. Murray, P. Bidwell, D. Ogilvy,

F. Fenton, S. Clegg. Middle row: M. Ruck, J. Gough, R. Kells, T. Priday (Captain), S. Barnes, J. Gibbs, F. Freeman. Front row: R. Lowe, G. Wells.

Sports days are as important as team matches and families often come to give their support. The story goes that in the 1940s a noble don with a large family attended a Sports day and asked the Headmaster: 'Excuse me, but could you please tell me which are mine?' It is indicative of the fact that dons often worked in their rooms in college, away from much of the minutiae of family life. Cricket is a particularly popular game. In 1931 the Big School played the Baby School and the report of the match in *The Draconian* (school magazine) highlights the efforts of two of the girls, namely Corinna Blackwell, who was praised for her perseverance, and Jane Galbraith (see Families) for bowling out one of the star batsmen. Girls also play rugger.

The Wind Band at the Dragon School in 1997, taken on School House lawn. (Courtesy the Dragon School and Gillman and Soame.) The girls are in their summer uniform and the boys in summer 'B-suits'. Back row, left to right:

M. Quartley, H. Synge, A Townsend, C. Andrewes, O. Darlington, H. Williams, D. Fox. Middle row: J. Bulstrade, A. Seaman, R. Judge, J. Agass, G. Henneker-Major, G. Adams, N. Hardy. Front (seated on chairs): R. Riddell, S. Hardy, T. Williams, C. Wallop, R. Logan, E. Fuller, C. Stewart. On the grass: S. Chance, E. Martin-Sperry and C. O'Regan.

The academic work of the Dragon, which takes boarders and day boys, has always been good with scholarships gained at the major Public Schools. In 1977, their Centenary year, they won both the top scholarships at Eton and Winchester. At one time pupils' marks, form place and full addresses appeared in *The Draconian.*

In her book *Loves and Labours,* Peggy Jay writes that her son Peter (later Ambassador to the USA) told her that life at the Dragon (in 1946) was 'tougher than anything he experienced later, even during his National Service on the lower deck of the Navy.' From 1938, 'Hum' Lynam, Skipper's younger brother, took over as Head and 'Hum's son Joc followed in 1956.

The Dragon School song ends with the words:

> *So they think of the days of their youth*
> *And they drain to the dregs of the flagon,*
> *To the school-house afar on the banks of the Cher,*
> *And the health of the conquering Dragon.*

The Oxford High School for Girls

The High School for Girls (Girls Public Day School Trust) was founded in 1875 and moved from St Giles to 21 Banbury Road (left) in 1880. The house had been erected in 1879 to the designs of Sir Thomas Jackson. Between 1887 and 1896, Lewis Carroll (the Reverend Charles Ludwidge Dodgson) gave logic lessons to the girls, finding them so 'bright and eager'. By 1888 there were 240 girls there. The building is now used by the University Department of Metallurgy. In 1945 the High School became a Direct Grant School and in 1976 an independent school. (Photograph taken in 1997.)

Tudor musicians at the High School in 1949 for a production of *Twelfth Night*. Music has always been an important part of the school's life and these unique pipes were made by the girls. Left to right: Bridget Senior, Jennifer Schurrock, Shiela Robinson, Christine McCallum.

The sixth form at the High School in 1952. The two back rows include Anne Theobald, Joyce Williams, Bridget Creed, Tessa Collins, Julie Pink, Heather Barrett, Catherine Mobey, Randa al Khaledi, Pat Walton, Barbara Beesley, Ruth Ayres, Josephine Morris, Barbara McCallum, Kathleen Dunkley, Yvonne Liddington, Alison Smith. Second row, left to right: Shiela Kempster (kneeling), Miss Tilston, Miss Bartholomew, Miss Mather, Margaret Slater. Front row: Audrey Wood, Pauline Treadwell, Bridget Senior. (The above two photographs courtesy of Mrs Bridget Davidson.)

The present buildings of the Oxford High School (1997) at the corner of Charlbury and Belbroughton Roads which have been their home since 1957. The buildings were designed by Stanley Ramsay and were officiallly opened by the Duchess of Gloucester in 1958. The school has high academic standards. Peter Snow in *Oxford Observed,* (1991) described it as a 'ferocious academic hothouse'. 'It is said to matter', he wrote, 'not if you go to University but *where.'*

Before the school was built there was a path leading from the end of Charlbury Road, through Gee's Nursery Gardens (later Tuckers) to Marston Ferry which crossed the river to the Victoria Arms at Marston. It was a popular walk for local people.

This outdoor heated swimming pool at the High School was provided as a leaving present to Miss V.E. Stack who was Headmistress from 1937 to 1959. The money was raised by past and present pupils and staff, parents and local governors in gratitude for her distinguished service. The Sunflower Swimming Club was formed which enables children and adults connected with the school to swim there during the summer holidays. (Photograph taken in August 1997.)

Wychwood School

Wychwood in 1911, then known as Miss Batty's School. She and Miss Lee (joint founders) are seen in this photograph. The school was started in 1897 with some 15 girls being taught at 77 Banbury Road (see North Parade). It had several other homes before its present, and permanent, one at 74 Banbury Road (from 1918). Later it took over No. 72, known as Sir John's House. It is an independent school for girls between 11 and 18 years and has been registered as an Educational Trust since 1952. Back row, left to right: M. Lock, Cynthia Driver, Janet Allen, S. Trevelyan, A. Burrows, Carola Oman, Joanna Cannan, S. Wilkinson, G. Eales. Third row: B. Conway, N. Gotch, A. Moss, R. Tideman, May Cannan, P. Thomson, Dulce Oman, Sylvia Driver, I. Murray, F. Eales. Second row: Miss Locock, Miss Margaret L. Lee (Joint Head), Miss Anne S. Batty (Joint Head), Mlle Ratoret, M. Godley, Miss Doering, Miss Rogers, J. Thatcher. Front row: R. Turner, J. Trevelyan, Beatrice Madan, B. Kranich, D. Eales, E. Jacks, C. Mackenzie, A. Cooper.

For over 75 years Wychwood has had a system of self-government with a school council consisting of staff and girls within a framework of democratic discussion. The Council is shown here in 1922 with a girl reading an account of her weekly form meeting.

The tennis court at Wychwood in 1922 against a background of 74 Banbury Road. The grass was later replaced by a hard surface. (Photographs courtesy of the School.)

Wychwood Centenary celebrations in July 1997 with tables and chairs on the tennis court. The two houses, No. 74 (right) and Sir John's, No. 72 (left) are joined by a modern addition with the library on the second floor.

Greycotes School

Greycotes School (founded 1929) in 1931. The founder, Mrs Norman Cunliffe, is seen in the middle of the second row in a long-sleeved dress, together with some of her staff. It is an independent day preparatory school for boys and girls. In 1997 there were 227 pupils aged 3–11 years but changes will take place by the turn of the century when it is fully amalgamated with the Oxford High School for Girls. Mrs Cunliffe started her school at her home in Holywell and then in Upland Park Road as early as 1926 but when 'Cherwell Croft' became available a 'real school' was able to be established there. The uniform consisted of grey kilt, white blouse and grey blazer and the felt hat had a pink cockade on the left. In the summer there were cotton frocks, white with blue sprigged flowers, and a panama hat. (Courtesy of Greycotes School.)

No. 1 Bardwell Road, designed by H.W. Moore (1891) where Greycotes has been since 1970. The site of 'Cherwell Croft' was developed by St John's College, the owners, and is now Cunliffe Close, named after the Greycotes founder. (See also Wartime section.)

The Crescent School

The cast of a Nativity play by the children of the Crescent (Froebel) School in the 1960s. It was at 7 Norham Gardens until the lease expired and was for boys and girls aged 3–11 years. They moved to a school in Richards Lane on the Woodstock Road called 'Cranescourt', keeping the name. This closed in about 1995.

Institutions

There are many educational institutions of note in North Oxford.

Wolsey Hall

Founded in Cirencester in 1894, Wolsey Hall moved to Oxford in 1907 where the Hall was on the site of Christ Church memorial garden. It moved to Banbury Road in 1930. A large new wing was added in 1961. It provides what used to be known as correspondence courses (now known as distance learning), some external University degrees and business and professional qualifications. The building was sold in 1989 to a Japanese educational trust called Technos International College which restored the building to its former glory, using the expert local firm of Symm's to repair the stonework. For this it was awarded an Oxford Preservation Trust plaque. Technos lease the building to Wolsey Hall and the Oxford English Centre and the Oxford Computer Group.

Wolsey Hall, 66 Banbury Road. The building was designed by Codd.

The Hall was one of the first of the many institutions, both educational and secretarial, or involved in language tuition which have established themselves in North Oxford. Others include the Oxford Language Centre School of English at 108 Banbury Road and the Swan School of English, 111 Banbury Road. D'Overbroek's College, Edward Greene's Tutorial Establishment, is at 1 Park Town. Students can join this coeducational establishment as early as 13. Its predecessor, 'Beech Lawn', was founded in 1947 by Miss J. Keays Young, who was very much a North Oxford character, in order to coach girls for Oxford and Cambridge entrance.

Maison Française

Maison Française, an institution of considerable prestige (right, photograph taken in 1997), was opened in June 1948 under the directorship of its founder, Henri Fluchère and established by the French Government. Fluchère (1898–1987), a scholar and translator was one of the most popular and memorable figures in post-war Oxford. He had an Honorary Doctorate from Oxford and an Honorary C.B.E. The Annual Garden Party at the Maison was one of Oxford's most popular social occasions.

Prime Minister Harold Macmillan arriving at the site of the new building of Maison Française to lay the foundation stone, in June 1962, with bedel and proctors.

Macmillan speaking at the laying of the foundation stone. Until 1963 Maison Française was at 72 Woodstock Road. (Both photographs courtesy of Madame Fluchère.)

The North Oxford Overseas Centre

The Centre, at 117 Banbury Road, is very much part of the North Oxford scene and gives a happy Christian welcome to students from abroad who are in Oxford to pursue courses, graduate degrees and so on. The photographs show a welcome party at the Centre in October 1997.

The Overseas Centre once owned No. 119, now Thackley End, which was acquired by the University. This was built on the site of the home of Professor and Mrs Wright. Joseph (Joe) Wright (1855–1930) began work as a donkey boy at the age of six and taught himself to read and write. He studied philology at Heidelberg University where he got his Ph.D. His greatest achievement was the *English Dialect Dictionary*. At Oxford he became Corpus Christi Professor of Comparative Philology, (1901–24). Among his friends and colleagues were James Murray and J.R.R. Tolkien (see Families), the latter being much attracted to Wright's teachings. In the 1930s and 1940s, Mrs Wright was a familiar bent figure in black walking her small, brown dog through the roads of North Oxford. She survived her husband for many years. The attractive and interesting house which he designed himself at 119 Banbury Road was sadly demolished for Thackley End.

There are a considerable number of University departments in North Oxford and it is not possible to illustrate or mention them all. One of the first (in 1914) was the Department of Engineering at the junction of Parks Road and Norham Gardens which was built on the site of Bates's Nursery. The University Department of Educational Studies at 15 Norham Gardens (built in 1871–3 by Codd) is one of the longest established. Others have been mentioned in the Buildings Section. Most of the Italianate villas at 17–19 Banbury Road house the University Computing Service and were fortunately saved from demolition. The vast University so-called 'Triangle' development (built on the Keble Road triangle) replaced a row of mid-19th century houses.

The Department of Engineering Science in Banbury Road. One only has to look at this building to imagine what much of southern North Oxford would have looked like if it had not been made a Conservation area. John Betjeman, in an article in the *Oxford Mail* in 1968, wrote about this building: 'The University, with a crassness only known to dons, has smashed into what was a Sylvan landscape with that concertina which is no doubt good of its kind but which would look more at home in Cowley.'

The Church

St Giles Church in the 1920s from Keble Road. (P.S.Spokes). Note the building on the right which was demolished in the 1960s. St Giles, to whom the Church is dedicated, lived in a remote area and when a church was first built on this site, thought to be in the 12th century, it would have been much isolated from other buildings. It was initially the centre of a large parish from the Cherwell in the east to Walton Street in the west and from St Giles northwards to Summertown. The church is mainly 13th century but was damaged in the Civil War. It had a major reconstruction in 1838. (See also Buildings section.)

The south part of Northmoor Road in the 1930s looking north with St Andrew's Church in the background. (Copyright Oxford Stamp Centre.)

St Andrew's Church today, taken in 1997 from the north-west. The parish was carved out of part of that of St Philip and St James in 1905, there having been many requests over a period of five years for an evangelical church in North Oxford, and there were long, drawn-out negotiations before the church got off the ground. A temporary iron church was there from 1905 until the new church was erected in 1906. The architect was Arthur Fenning who pressed strongly for the Norman style. There had been plans for a tower to the north but it was never built. A pleasant and useful church room, more attractive inside than out, was added in 1988. The application for this was turned down twice by the City Planning Committee, some suggesting that it would look like a cricket pavilion, greenhouse or tea room. In this photograph Mrs J.R. Seyer, who lives in the house on the right, is posting a letter.

The Church room at St Andrew's is much used and is particularly popular in an area with little community provision. Many parents bring their toddlers for play and socialising. The group here have moved from the church room into the church for a singing session (1997). Back row, left to right: Linda Erin with Gabriel Erin, Charlotte Broomfield with (left) Tobias and Bethany Broomfield, Anne Richter, Kim O'Brien with Matthew O'Brien, Henri Connell with Henry Connell, Katerina Kolosova with Ksenia. Front row: Jake Halsey (on floor behind unidentified child), Carol Petersen with (right) Augustin and Magnus, Jill Collett with Cleminte Collett.

Kenneth Escott Kirk, Regius Professor of Moral and Pastoral Theology and Bishop of Oxford from 1937. He died in office in 1954. His wife Beatrice died in 1934, leaving five young children. They are seen here in 1924 with Hilary (18 months) and Joan (6 months).

Four of the five Kirk children in the 1920s ready for a swim. Left to right: Peter, Pat, Joan and Hilary. Roger is not in the photograph. The family lived at 10 Norham Road from 1921 to 1930 and then at 21 Norham Gardens until 1934 when they moved to Christ Church.

The Bishop of Oxford's house in Linton Road. Bishop Patrick and Mrs Rodger lived here from 1978 to 1987 and it is now the home of the present Bishop Richard Harries and Dr Harries and family. (Taken in 1997.)

Wycliffe Hall, founded in 1877, is at 54 Banbury Road, the house built for Thomas Arnold, son of the great Head of Rugby School. The house became vacant when the Hall, Evangelical Anglican, was looking for premises. It is a training college for Anglican clergy and became part of the University in 1996. It can now take undergraduates studying theology. The Hall owns many houses nearby including No. 2a (Principal's house) Norham Gardens, Nos. 2 and 5 Norham Gardens and No. 4 is used by them. Single students live in and married ones live out. The group was taken in 1889 in front of Wycliffe Hall as a farewell picture for Canon Girdlestone. Back row, left to right: M. Jaulmes, Canon Girdlestone (first Principal), C.C. im Thurn, E.H. Horne, A. Daunt, S.T. Dawson. Middle row: Mrs Girdlestone, C.B. Harrison, Rev. J. Hewetson, C.H. Coles, A.G.C. Ewing. Front row: T.W. Pritchard, Gaythorne Girdlestone (who became a well-known medical man and was the founder of the Wingfield (now Nuffield) Orthopaedic Centre), J.A. Large, W.I. Moran.

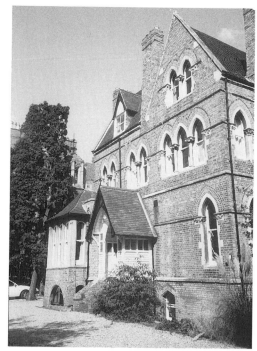

Wycliffe Hall as it is today (1997).

The Orthodox Church in Canterbury Road was built in 1972–73. The Russian Orthodox parish in Oxford goes back to the early 1940s and later they worshipped in a room at St Gregory's House, 1 Canterbury Road, from 1959 until 1973. The Greek Orthodox parish (in existence since 1966) and the Russian parish agreed to build the new Church and it is shared on an equal footing between the two. There are two Bishops, Bishop Kallistos of Diklia (Greek Orthodox) and Bishop Basil of Sergievo (Russian Orthodox).

Health

Opening of the Acland Home (25 Banbury Road) by the Prince of Wales (later King Edward VII) standing (right) in top hat, in May 1897, the same day on which he opened the new Town Hall. Doctor Sir Henry Acland F.R.S. (1815–1900), in a wheelchair, was Honorary Physician to the Prince and accompanied him to America in 1860. The Home (now a Hospital) was built in memory of Acland's wife, Sarah, who died in 1878. Acland was a distinguished physician and academic, a Fellow of All Souls, Radcliffe Librarian and Aldrichian Professor of Clinical Medicine, Regius Professor of Medicine and President of the General Medical Council. It was during his Presidency that he was influential in persuading the Council and Queen Victoria to accept women as doctors. He was a life-long friend of John Ruskin who supported Acland in his plans for the University Museum. As a doctor he treated anyone who was anybody and was well-loved by both Town and Gown. In the Oxford great cholera epidemic of 1854 he took a leading role in the relief measures and the necessary improvements in sanitation. The original building was designed by Sir Thomas Jackson. A new wing was added in 1937, made possible by a gift from Lord Nuffield. It was designed by Fielding Dodd who also added a new front. In 1962, the Nuffield Nursing Homes Trust took over the running of the hospital. Further addtions were built in 1979. (Photograph courtesy of Nuffield Nursing Homes Trust.)

St Luke's Nursing Home was originally situated here at 20 Linton Road from 1957 until it moved to Headington in 1982. It was founded and led by Mrs Mary McMaster (née Neville) who had worked for ten years with Mr Girdlestone and was keen that St Luke's should specialise in rehabilitation. She started in a small way with a vision in 1953 and began fund-raising with only £1 in the kitty. In 1963 Mary Neville married Ian McMaster who was able to help her considerably in the development of St Luke's. St John's sold the freehold to Wolfson College. The building is now the Centre for Socio-Legal Studies. (Photograph taken in 1997.)

The British Red Cross Society, Oxfordshire Branch, was founded in 1909. By 1915 the Branch was running and staffing nine Voluntary Aid Detachment (V.A.D.) hospitals including Felstead House in Banbury Road. The first typewriter was purchased for the office in 1917 for £16. The first office was in Keble Road when, in 1944, a larger place was required. They heard that the lease of 41 St Margaret's Road was for sale and approached prominent people for donations. Lord Nuffield replied that he did not like subscribing to specific projects but was ready to donate £3,000. As this was the cost of the lease the Red Cross responded with alacrity. In the photograph with Lord Nuffield at the official opening in May, 1944 are the Duchess of Marlborough (right) and Mrs Foxley-Norris.

In 1948, jointly with the WRVS, they started the meals-on-wheels service. They also ran an Old People's Home at 107 Banbury Road and began their medical loan department.

No. 101 Banbury Road, the present headquarters of the Oxfordshire Branch of the British Red Cross Society (taken in 1997). The Oxfordshire Branch was the first in the country to employ a fully-qualified social worker, Miss P.E. White. The present building was bought for £17,000 in 1951. An extension was built in 1966. (Information kindness of Mr Michael Page and 1944 photograph courtesy of British Red Cross.)

Shopping

North Parade

It is hard to think what North Oxford would do without North Parade even though nowadays it is not as it used to be — the main shopping area for residents of the neighbourhood. Only a few villas had been built on the 'cockhorse road' to Banbury in the 1830s when Richard Carr developed North Parade. Many have puzzled over the fact that North Parade is south of South Parade, Summertown but Summertown and its Parade were developed much later. It is only a myth that it had something to do with the Civil War parade grounds for the troops.

At the entrance to North Parade, at the corner of Banbury Road, stands 77 Banbury Road, built in about 1840 and listed (Grade II) of architectural and historical merit. (Photograph taken in 1997.)

North Parade looking west with the spire of St Philip and St James in the background. Before the church was built, North Parade was a cul de sac. The buildings in North Parade are mainly freehold. The photograph was taken in 1997 from the tower of Wolsey Hall. (Courtesy Oxford English Centre.)

North Parade, westward view from the top floor of 77 Banbury Road (courtesy of the present owners) July 1997.

At one time the Parade shops satisfied most needs of North Oxford families who were able to go there on foot or by bicycle. Meat, fish, fresh fruit and vegetables, groceries, dairy products, furniture, ironmongery, boots and shoes, books and stationery, confectionary and bicycle accessories and repairs were all found there.

A shopping bag from Rouse, the fishmongers. The brothers Rouse were big and jovial in their white caps and white overalls. During the Second World War one of the brothers was called up and was replaced by their sister Rosie who was buxom and friendly and stood outside the shop, as fishmongers always did, slapping the wet fish about.

(Alfred) Cecil Walker in 1988.

The Walkers. Walker's the ironmongers was also full of advice on household matters. Miss Withycombe (on tape borrowed from Mrs P. Smith) recalled consulting them when the strawberry jam would not set.

Miss Withycombe also remembered that many of the traders only had one child, or at most two, who were given a good education and usually went into a profession. Until the end of the 1940s North Parade really was for shopping with no boutiques, restaurants or launderettes. The pubs, the Rose and Crown and the Gardener's Arms, still remain though, old favourites as they are. (Photograph courtesy of Mr A. Walker.)

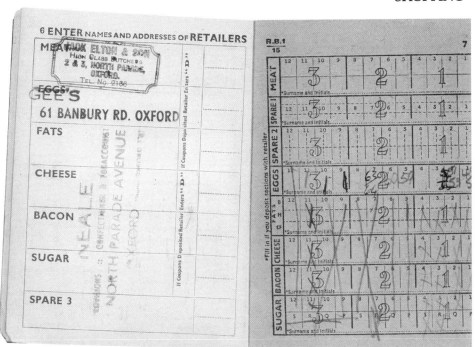

Part of a war-time ration book owned by a North Oxford resident. Note Elton the butcher, Neale, provisions, and Gee's for eggs, stamped on the book. Before Mr Elton came, the butcher was Mr Huggins who always used to wear leather gaiters and a bowler hat with his butcher's blue and white striped apron. He was one of the last in England to drive his own horse and cart. His wife did the accounts and dealt with the ration books. Some people found war-time shopping like the pleasures of the chase as one never knew what one would come home with. Some would join a queue even if they did not know what it was for.

Right: Mr Huggins with his horse. Left: Mrs Huggins. (Courtesy of Mr Bob Jeffries.)

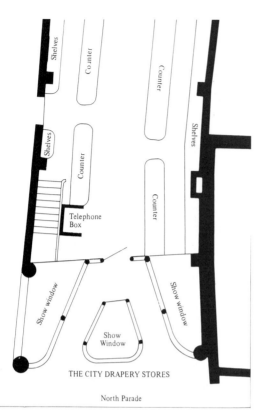

THE CITY DRAPERY STORES

North Parade

Plan of the interior of the City Drapery Stores, 1903. It was at 1 North Parade. Note the telephone box. (Courtesy Mr R.J. Earl.)

As will be seen from the signboard, some like to call the road North Parade Avenue. Miss Margaret Lee, an Oxford University don and the Head of Wychwood School, who lived for many years at No. 77 (the house seen in the background), was heard to object in 1936: 'It merely excites ridicule because no one ever calls it that.' Such tautology is not for academics.

The Post-Office in North Parade with the present joint proprietor, Mrs Elaine Newbold. Once Ora's sweet shop, it has been patronised by generations of local children, Dragons and Wychwood girls. John Betjeman, when he was at the Dragon school in 1916 would often visit Ora Brown, the 'cheerful lady who sold sweets.' In the 1920s and 1930s it was a treasure house of brightly-coloured gob-stoppers in large glass bowls, temptingly placed at child height, chocolate creams and bars, liquorice allsorts, fudge, wine gums and turkish delight. One could choose boiled sweets from a long line of glass jars which were taken down from the shelves and tilted up so that one's order could be weighed on the scales and then placed in white paper bags, twisted at each corner. One could buy a bottle of pop for three farthings. At one time the Post Office was round the corner in Banbury Road at Slatter and Rose, newsagents.

Two views of Gee's taken in August, 1997. It is now a restaurant but was once a popular fruit and flower shop of the same name. Originally, Mr Gee, nurseryman, set up his shop to supply the new North Oxford gardens with shrubs and plants. Mavis Batey, the garden historian, author of *Oxford Gardens,* writes: 'ferns and spikey plants in pots to echo spikey finials and gables were much in demand' as were the specialised carnations sold by Joseph Bates, who set up the Parks Nursery by the University Parks near the new Victorian suburb. Note the surviving iron railings. The very neat and ladylike Mrs Pike (née Gee) who wore her her hair in a bun, and her son, ran the famous shop for many years. Here were made up the wedding bouquets and funeral wreaths for generations of North Oxford families.

Elliston and Cavell

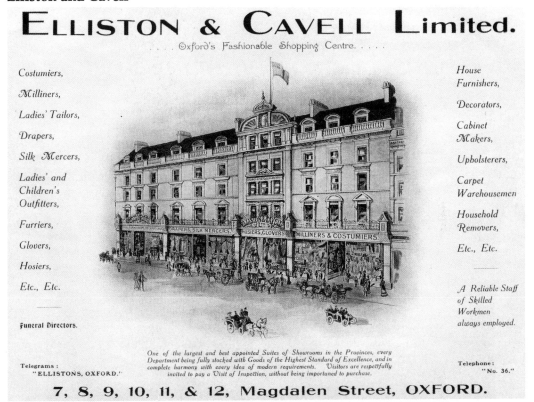

Elliston and Cavell Ltd (taken over in 1953 by Debenham's) in Magdalen Street which was frequented by North Oxford families from its early days. It was founded by Jesse Elliston in 1823 as a draper's store and he was joined by James Cavell in 1835. The architects were H.G.W. Drinkwater and M.V. Treleaven. The facade will fortunately remain after major development in 1998. It is said that only the wives of Heads of Houses and Professors could enter the front door of Elliston's from their carriages. Everybody else had to enter from the side. Note the carriages and single automobile in this drawing of about 1910. Once dons were allowed to marry, from 1877 onwards, the young dons' wives, influenced by Ruskin and Walter Pater, wore loose smocks and shapeless garments which were hand-embroidered with sunflowers and marigolds, together with long amber necklaces. Morris wallpapers and liberty cretonnes were also popular. This meant that those traders who had relied on the fashions of the time had to change their ideas and become up-to-date.

Transport and Communications

Transport

*'When we had donned our Liberty gowns we went out to dinner,
the husband walking, the wife in a bath chair, drawn by an ancient
member of an ancient and close fraternity, the chairmen of Oxford.'*

Mrs Humphrey Ward

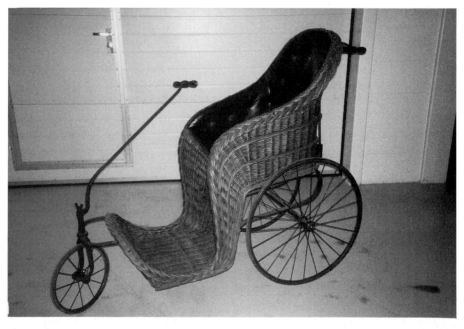

Bath chairs were a popular means of transport before cars and when ladies' long dresses meant that walking to dinners and parties was not feasible. The 1852 County Directory lists nine bath chair hirers in Oxford. Because they were allowed right into the quads of colleges one could go door to door for dinner and keep one's feet dry. Above is a typical bath chair similar to those used in North Oxford. (Photograph taken courtesy of Oxfordshire Museums Store.)

A man friend of a female undergraduate could walk beside the chair which the chair man would push, thus avoiding the need for a chaperone. The occupant would steer. Miss Wordsworth, Principal of LMH, would often go by bath chair to dine in Oxford. Annie Rogers told the story of the time Christ Church undergraduates ran bath chair races in the quad (when presumably the bath chair men were taking refreshment elsewhere) and they even pushed them up the staircase to Hall. On one occasion the bottom fell out of a chair and the hapless hirer had to walk back home with the sides of the chair around her. Even children went to parties in bath chairs and there was a double chair, which was in great demand, in which a whole family of children could be fitted.

A horse and cab were a popular means of transport until the arrival of the motor car. Brewer's Mews, behind Fyfield Road was where the wealthy people of Norham Manor kept their horses and carriages. Mrs Brewer ran a cab hire business from her home at the Mews entrance. In the 1920s when cars replaced horses the North Oxford ladies begged that Mr Cook, the oldest cab driver, and his white horse should be kept on until their retire-

ment and promised to use them. A fly, as seen above, was any one-horse covered carriage like a cab or hansom let out for hire from a livery stable.

Once the first Principal of Somerville, Miss Shaw Lefevre, soon after her arrival, ordered a fly to take her to dinner with the Vice-Chancellor at Pembroke College. When it did not arrive she had to run through the rain, arriving just in time. (Photograph courtesy Oxford Stamp Centre.)

Goods were delivered to homes by horse-drawn vans or by errand boys on bicycles with vast baskets on the front.

Horse trams were introduced in Oxford in 1881 after the Oxford Tramways Order and Tramways Act were passed. In January 1882, a service up the Banbury Road as far as St Margaret's Road was inaugurated. It started at Carfax and then went via Cornmarket and St. Giles. The photograph was taken about 1900. The conductor is standing with the driver in front of the horses. Trams were replaced by motor buses in about 1914. (Copyright Oxford Stamp Centre.)

A bullnose Morris of the 1920s from a contemporary advertisement. Oxford's chronic traffic problem began early. In 1925 a Town Planning scheme stated that drivers should be asked to leave their cars outside the City centre. Through traffic was also a continual problem even then.

A Morris Cowley car of later date. Note the registration letters FC. Other letters allocated to Oxford were JO and WL. (Copyright Jeremy's Postcards.)

The Kirks (see The Church) hired a bus for holidays from their home at 10 Norham Rd (demolished for Maison Française). (This 1926 photograph by courtesy of Joan Clarke.)

Wychwood schoolgirls about to leave for their annual outing to Wychwood Forest in a charabanc. The concertina hood at the back could be pulled forward if it rained. (Courtesy Wychwood School.)

Bicycles have always been an essential possession for North Oxford residents and undergraduates alike. This photograph was taken in 1931 and shows (left to right) Penelope Stradling (see Families), Ruth Marle, Rachel Stradling and Mardie Galloway, outside 1 Charlbury Road. (Courtesy Mrs R. Blaney.)

Communications

1895

LIST OF SUBSCRIBERS

TO THE

OXFORD EXCHANGE.

CALL OFFICES.

46	1, NORTH PARADE	City Drapery Stores
20	54, CORNMARKET STREET ...	National Telephone Co., Ltd.

A

33 ALDEN, R. R., The Market
37 ALDEN, R. R., Eastwick Farm
43 ALINGTON, REV. E. H.
83 ALL SOULS' COLLEGE (Porter's Lodge)
83a ALL SOULS' COLLEGE (C. G. Robertson)
67 AXTELL, THOS., 9a, St. Aldates
67a AXTELL, THOS., Edith Road, Grandpont

B

30 BAKER, HILL & Co., 1, Broad Street
30a BAKER, HILL & Co. (E. L. Birkbeck Hill), 59, St. Giles
30b BAKER, HILL & Co., 9 & 10, George Street

70 BALLIOL COLLEGE (Porter's Lodge)
44 BATES, J.
45 BEAUMONT, E., 10, 11, & 12, High Street
46 BEAUMONT, E. (Call Office), 1, North Parade
38 BEVERS, E. A., M.R.C.S., and L.S.A. Lond.
80 BODLEIAN LIBRARY
62 BROOKS, W. T., M.D.
2 BUTLER, A., The Market
2a BUTLER, A., 153, Cowley Road

C

59 CAB STAND, St. Giles
76a CANNAN, C.
24 CARFAX COAL EXCHANGE
47 CARTER, MESSRS.
45 CITY DRAPERY STORES, 10, 11 & 12, High Street

A telephone list (books came later) in 1895. Note the call office in the City Drapery Stores (see North Parade). Trades people, cab stands, colleges, libraries and hospitals were some of the first to install telephones. As both City and University were against overhead wires, it was agreed in 1898 to put tubes for cables under the roads. By 1899 there were 25 Oxford subscribers.
(Courtesy of Mr R.A.J. Earl.)

Below left: A typical telephone of 1924. The first automatic exchange was not opened until 1926 and before that time people had to go through the exchange even for local calls. North Oxford beyond St Margaret's Road was included in the Summertown exchange.

Below right: A more modern looking telephone of 1929. (Both telephone photographs by courtesy of Mr R.A.J. Earl.)

The University and colleges have been permitted to run a messenger service for correspondence since 1656.

Between 1871 and 1886, when the postmaster-General banned their use, some of the colleges issued their own stamps. Seen above are those of, left to right: Lincoln, Hertford, Merton and All Souls.

The University Messengers in 1998. Left to right: Roger King, Harry Cook, Michael Dyer (Head), Brian Greer, Ken Eaton.

The Service collects from and delivers to University Departments and delivers to colleges which also have their own services. The University Service developed in its present form in 1976.

North Oxford in Wartime

In the First World War many North Oxford families suffered the tragic loss of their young men — 'the flower of Britain's youth'. There were also losses in the Second World War but not to the same extent. Oxford was fortunate not to be the target of bombers during wartime although there was an accident involving a British plane. A Whitley bomber crashed in North Oxford in May 1941 and landed on 'Cherwell Lodge', a cottage in the grounds of 'Cherwell', the Haldane home, fatally wounding the owner, Mrs Hitchcox, and with the loss of the three RAF crew.

A First World War wedding. Henry Edgeworth Butler married Margaret Lucy Pollard on 3rd November 1917. Left to right: Mrs Alice Lucy, grandmother of the bride (of Lucy's Ironworks), Henry E. Butler, Professor Albert Frederick Pollard, Fellow of All Souls (at back), Margaret L. Pollard, Morris Fitzgerald, best man (at back), Mrs Harriet Jessie Butler (widow of Arthur G. Butler and mother of the groom), Dr W.A. Spooner (who married the couple and made one of his few spoonerisms during the service, saying: 'Ye who are loifully jawned together'), Mrs A.F. Pollard (née Lucy), the bride's mother. The bride wished to be married in her VAD nurse's uniform (after all, her husband was wearing his Army uniform) but neither her mother or future mother-in-law would allow it. Nevertheless, she managed to make herself look a bit like a nurse. (Courtesy of Christina Colvin.)

Oxford City Civil Defence Wardens' Service, Area C, North Oxford, 1939–45 War. (Courtesy of Gilman and Soame).

An Air Raid Warden. Peter Spokes, Sector Warden, showing the full uniform and boots. (Taken in March 1945.)

At first, in the Second World War the only uniform for Wardens was a tin hat. Then, when the full uniform was issued, the ladies pondered whether they would opt for a skirt or trousers as a choice was offered. Some North Oxford ladies had never worn trousers before and there was a great discussion among them as to what they would choose. Some were still undecided when they reported to the Police Station in Blue Boar Street where they were issued with the uniform and some even asked the Sergeant (on duty with two Constables) what he advised. As one practice exercise involved crawling on hands and knees under a smoke screen, trousers were obviously more practical. They could also be put on hurriedly over pyjamas.

Miss Betty Withcombe, one of the younger Wardens who was attached to what she called our 'genteel' ARP post, said that, despite the fact that the Butler sisters were 'born on bicycles', Violet, used to riding in a long skirt, could not stay on her bicycle in trousers and fell off.

Petrol was strictly rationed and many people laid up their cars 'for the duration'. However, a special allocation of petrol was issued to people coming home on leave from the Forces. Lady Mott, wife of Sir Adrian, who lived at 20 Charlbury Road, applied for her husband's allocation. Despite his baronetcy he preferred to serve as a Private in the Army and only a small amount — about a gallon or so — was issued to Privates. One day Lady Mott came home to find about ten gallons of petrol stacked in their driveway addressed to 'General Sir Adrian Mott.'

One of the Air Raid Warden posts was at St Hugh's college. Here a diary was kept and comments inserted, some of which may seem trivial compared with the momentous events elsewhere. Typical are examples such as:

'Light bulb not working. Please supply new one.'

'Floor filthy, needs sweeping.'

'Floor still a disgrace. Can't something be done?'

This was followed next day by the entry:

'Brought broom and swept floor', signed Lady Young.

Another Air Raid post was at 'Gunfield', Norham Gardens, the home of the Misses Deneke, situated near their kitchen. Miss M. Deneke, the 'Queen of Oxford music', often slept on the bed in the post. She had decided that her 'war work' would be making her own bed. Never having done this before she was not very good at it and some of the other ladies were shocked when they could see things under the bed. The Deneke's housekeeper was embarrassed and felt it let the house down.

There were many academic Wardens, three or four Professors and tutors, and many were rather old. If the siren went everyone had to report for duty and Wardens would patrol on foot in pairs. Sometimes they were out all night, night after night. Oxford was on the outer defences of London, Bristol and the Midlands which bore the brunt of the enemy air raids. Betty Withycombe remembered that Wardens were supposed to look out for 'butterfly' bombs but nobody knew what they looked like and patrolling the streets of the Norham area with its big houses and large gardens it was impossible to see what fell. She and some others spent nights on Wolsey Hall tower where they could see more of what was going on. One of their duties was to make sure that the blackout curtains were effective enough to keep out any light. Miss Lorimer, a very academic lady, once invited the hostess of the St Anne's hostel at 13 Norham Gardens to come outside on a nasty November evening and lie down in the shubbery in order to be shown that there was a narrow chink of light showing. When the hostess thought it unlikely that any airman could see it she was told that it must be '100% perfect'. Even bicycles had to have their lights covered with two layers of tissue paper, by order.

The blackout had its benefits. The Librarian at St. Hugh's said 'Oxford was ravishing, the moonlight uncontaminated by street lighting.'

TEAR	C.A.P.	Sweet.	N.P.	Smarting & running	Respirators : bathe eyes with saline.
	K.S.K.	Fruity, pear drops	P.	eyes: can't keep	Reassure. B.B.C./K.S.K. also wash
	B.B.C.	Bitter sweet.	V.P.	open : panic.	nose and throat with bicarb. solution.
LUNG	Chlorine	Bleaching-powder smell.	N.P.	Choking, eye irrit-ation, sickness.	Respirator : get victim out of gas ;
	Phosgene*	Musty hay	N.P.	**Dangerous well-**	loosen clothes. **Rest in Recumbent**
	Diph'g'ne*	Musty hay	N.P.	**being after 1st effect.**	**Posture.**
BLISTER	Mustard	Garlic or mustard; action delayed.	V.P.	Eyes, skin, respira-tory passages	**Speed essential.** Wash eyes : bleach on skins : wipe fluid : swab with petrol : don't break blisters : remove
	Lewisite	Strong, pungt. geranium: action instant.	P.	affected.	contaminated clothing.
NOSE	D.A.	No smell:	Solid at ordy. temp.	Sneezing, pain in head, teeth, jaw, nose, throat, sickness.	Keep respirator on : gargle with bicarbonate, suck up nose, hot coffee or alcohol. Recovery 1 to
	D.M.	often invisible:			18 hours.
	D.C.	action delayed.			
ARSINE		Gas or white powder: no smell. Paper A.	N.P.	Poisons blood stream, cumulative.	Respirator: hot sweet tea: stretcher case : Doctor quickly.

Instructions issued to a North Oxford Warden in the Second World War about tear gas and how to treat it. The instruction: 'Keep respirator on and gargle with bicarbonate' might have been difficult to put to the test.

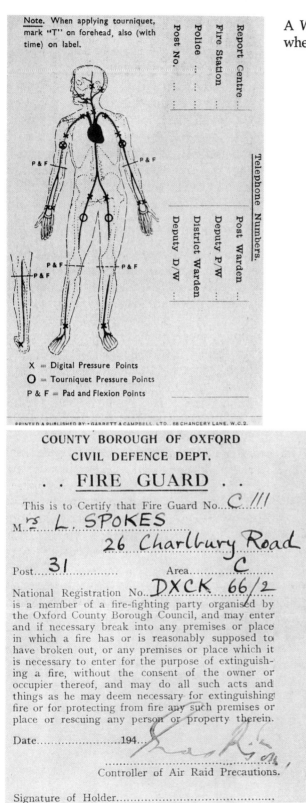

A Warden's instruction card, including where to apply a tourniquet.

A North Oxford Fire Guard's pass card which permitted her to break and enter any premises where a fire might have broken out in order to extinguish it. This would have been for a Fire Guard patrolling the streets. Also, large buildings had their Fire Guards. They were not strictly volunteers, though, as everyone connected with the building had to do regular fire-watching duty. Undergraduates were paid a shilling a night for fire-watching.

Oxford was crammed full of people during the war with various Government departments taking over the colleges. St Hugh's became a hospital for head injuries in the 1939–45 war.

The surgical and medical staff at the hospital in 1945. Back row, left to right: Capt. Harrington, Capt. Mackenzie, Capt. Northcroft, Major Phillips, (Australian neuro-surgeon), Capt. Guthkeltch, Capt. Gordon (Canadian), Capt. Collard, Capt. Rampling, Capt. Taverner, Major Smythe, Capt. Harrington, Major Henderson (neuro-surgeon), Major Kremer (neurologist), Capt. M. Graham (dental surgeon who made all the bone grafts), Capt. Small (neuro-surgeon). Major Danin (anaesthesist). Major Waite (radiologist). (Two on far right not identified.) Front row: Major Western (pathologist), Major C. Calvert, (Principal Assistant to the Brigadier), Brigadier Cairns, Colonel Roche (non-medical Chief of Military Personnel), Air Commodore Sir Charles Symonds, (Head of the Neurological Medical Department), Major Ritchie Russell (neurologist), Major Walkley (non-medical), Major Reynell (Psychiatrist).

The once beautiful gardens (see entry on St Hugh's) were covered with brick huts which were not demolished until 1952. The college was able to celebrate the gardens being restored to all their serene beauty in 1953.

School children also 'did their bit' in North Oxford in the Second World War. Here some Greycotes girls and their Headmistress, Mrs Cunliffe (seated) are seen after presenting special radio contact apparatus to a ship's company on 'secret missions'. The ship is not identified. (Courtesy of Greycotes School.

There were many shortages of food during the war, especially any which had to come from abroad. At the Oxford High School a single banana, which was suspended from the ceiling, was first prize in a raffle.

North Oxford looked very different once all its iron railings had been removed. Here men are collecting railings in 1942 when their salvage became compulsory. They were intended to be melted down to help the war effort but no record of this was undertaken. (Courtesy of Centre for Oxfordshire Studies.)

Families

To chronicle the history of every family who has lived in North Oxford at some time during the last century would take many volumes. I have therefore selected a sample of 26 — in some cases depending on the availability of photographs — which I hope will give an impression of the kind of people who have made their home in the Norham Manor area of North Oxford over the years.

There were many families I would have liked to include, especially the Chapmans, Creightons, Brett-Smiths, Gibbs, Greens, Gotchs, Huxleys, Lankesters, MacKinders, Gilbert Murrays, Paters, Prichards, Toynbees, Veales and Vernon Harcourts. I would also have liked space to include Iris Murdoch, Elizabeth Jennings and J.I.M. Stewart, representatives of North Oxford's rich literary life. Also a chapter on dinner parties and their rituals has had to be omitted because of lack of space. There is much also waiting to be written about voluntary work, the raising of children, life below stairs and beloved family pets.

The Adams Family

There have been three generations of Adams running hotels in North Oxford. George Adams (from Bladon) and his wife Emily ran 100 Banbury Road from the start of the Second World War until they changed it into apartments in the 1950s. It was in 1976 that Mrs Zelia Crockett (née Adams) and her husband changed it back to a hotel and named it 'Parklands'. Zelia is the grandaughter of George and Emily.

Meanwhile the son of George and Emily, with his wife Peggy, ran 87 Banbury Road as a popular hotel. When the lease of this expired in 1985 the building was taken over by St. Hugh's college.

The wedding of Zelia Adams and Alun Crockett, 1st June 1963. Left to right: Emily Adams, George Adams, Mrs Bronwen Crockett, John Crockett (with bridesmaid Sally Bruce in front), Miss Bronwen Crockett, David Powell (best man), Alun Crockett, Zelia Crockett (née Adams), Jill Adams, Hugh Adams, bridesmaid Jane Adams, Peggy Adams, Dorothy Wright and Cecil Wright.

Parklands Hotel, 100 Banbury Road (in 1997).

Both hotels have had many famous visitors. On one occasion two Rolls Royces drew up at Parklands and the Zimbabwean Ambassador asked to come in for a cup of tea. As a student he had lived there when it had been a guest house and he was delighted to meet a third generation of the Adams family.

The Bowens

The distinguished scientist Edmund John Bowen (1898–1980) (known as Ted) and his wife Edith began married life at 15 Banbury Road but moved to No. 10 (then No. 7) Park Town in 1934. They celebrated their golden wedding in 1974. They had two children, Margaret and Humphry.

Mrs Edith (Ede) Bowen, centre, and her daughter Margaret, aged nine months, in 1928. The car is a Riley. (Courtesy of Mrs M. Pinsent.)

Dr Bowen and his wife Edith with daughter Margaret (Mrs Pinsent), centre, and grandchildren (left) John Pinsent and (right) Jonathan Bowen at 10 Park Town, 28th April 1957. (Courtesy Mrs M. Pinsent.)

Dr Bowen, who became a Fellow of the Royal Society in 1935, was a pioneer in the study of photochemical reactions, especially in connection with fluorescence. His time at Balliol, where he won the Brackenbury scholarship at the age of 16½, was interrupted by the First World War. He was one of the fortunate ones who survived Ypres, Cambrai and the Somme. He returned in 1920 to Oxford where he spent the rest of his life. He later held the most senior post in his subject. In the Second World War he worked on respirator problems and was an Air Raid Warden. His Christmas lectures for children, with demonstrations, were colourful and popular. The Bowens have a continuity of academic tradition through four generations: Edmund Riley Bowen, his son Dr Edmund John Bowen, grandson Dr. Humphry John Moule Bowen and greatgrandson Jonathan Bowen: all teachers/lecturers with scientific interests and all practical carpenters. Other members of the family, both female and male, have been teachers and lecturers.

Margaret Pinsent (née Bowen) still lives at 10 Park Town, a home of some historic as well as architectural interest. One of its early occupants was Sarah Acland, daughter of Sir Henry Acland (see Health section). She was an important amateur photographer and recorded many of her father's friends in the 1890s such as the Marquis of Salisbury and W.E. Gladstone whom she described as 'a most kind and patient sitter.' She extended the house in 1903 in order to install up-to-date plumbing. She developed her own colour plates in a darkroom in the house. The turret on top of the house has panoramic views. In the garden is a splendid acer palmatum maple tree, the gift of a Japanese Professor to Miss Acland and there are two memorial gravestones of Miss Acland's dogs set in the garden wall.

An 1820 grate in the basement of 10 Park Town which was probably installed during the time of Miss Acland. It pre-dates the house which was built in 1854.

The Peveril grate in art nouveau style, made in 1904. (Photographs taken in 1997.)

The Browns

J.B. Brown (always known as Bruno), a name familiar to generations of Dragons, and his wife Helen (née Crabtree) in 1960. It was Bruno who produced the school's famous Gilbert and Sullivan productions from 1919 to 1962. Helen Brown was for many years an Independent member of Oxford City Council and a J.P. They had two children, David and June. Sadly, David was killed in a motor accident in 1940 at the age of 19 just before he was due to be called up into the Forces.

Bruno returned from War Service to take his degree at Oxford and then, in 1919, started teaching at the Dragon School. Married in 1920, they first lived in a school house full of boys at 10 Charlbury Road. It was here, in July 1925, that June (now Mrs Tom Soper) was born. The Dragon boys, delighted by the arrival of a baby, rushed off to the school tuck shop and bought her a present — a pennyworth of acid drops. (Photograph courtesy of Mrs June Soper.)

No. 26 Norham Road where the Browns lived from 1930 to 1973. It was ideally situated on the corner of Dragon Lane. Built in 1895, it looks much the same in 1998 except for the loss of its iron railings. The house is now the home of Mr and Mrs Hugo Brunner. He is Lord Lieutenant of Oxfordshire.

The Butlers

The Butlers lived at 14 Norham Gardens, a house which was designed by Codd and built in the 1860s for the Sackville Wests. The Hon. W.E. Sackville West was Bursar of Keble College and in order to cope with large dinner parties Codd had added a wing in 1874 containing a spacious dining-room.

Arthur Gray Butler (1831–1909) and his wife Harriet (who died in 1946 at the age of 92) came to Oxford in the late 1870s. It is said that whenever Arthur Butler came into a room people's faces would light up. He had been Headmaster at Haileybury. His older brother George married Josephine Butler, the social reformer. From 1856 to 1858 those Butlers ran Butler's Hall in Oxford.

A drawing of Arthur Butler by his daughter Olive, about 1900.

Arthur Butler was a Fellow of Oriel College and tutor there to Cecil Rhodes. It was at dinner in 1889 that Butler suggested to Rhodes, triumphant at just receiving an honorary Doctorate despite opposition, that Rhodes provide in his will for the augmentation of the salaries of Oriel fellows. He left them £100,000. Butler also wrote verse and drama.

Here are a few lines from one of his sonnets which he wrote on Rhodes:

'Deep voice, broad fronted with the Caesar's brow
A dreamer with a diamond in his hand . . .
Musing on Empire.'

The Butler sisters, Violet, Ruth and Olive. In about 1895, Lewis Carroll was interested in the Butler girls and came to visit them at 14 Norham Gardens. He was much taken with Olive (born 1879) who would have been about 16 at the time and he wanted her to go round to visit him at Christ Church. However, Olive's father would not allow it. Carroll was very hurt and in a note to Arthur said that only the Sidgwicks had ever refused.

Two contemporary photographs of the drawing-room at 14 Norham Gardens when the Arthur Butlers lived there. Note the Morris wallpaper and ornate legs on the oblong piano in the top picture and the ornate Gothic fireplace in the bottom one. The high, Queen Anne style, black oak overmantel was made for the house on the Butlers' instructions in 1881 and cost them £5.

Harriet Butler (widow of Arthur) with her son Harold (later Professor of Latin at University College, London) with the Nurse (right), known as 'Nanna' to the children. She came in 1878 when Harold was born and stayed with the Butlers until her death in 1929. Her name was Martha Elizabeth Bean Kirk.

Mabel, champion pastry maker and cook, and Mrs Scuce, family retainer for the Arthur Butler family, at 14 Norham Gardens.

Professor Harold Butler with some of his family. Left to right) Laurence Colvin (grandson), Christina Colvin (daughter), Harold Butler, Olive Butler, sister, with Hugh Colvin (grandson) and (at back) Violet Butler, sister. This was taken in about 1950 on the steps of 14 Norham Gardens.

Violet Butler on a swing in 1891. She was said to have been a naughty child.

Violet Butler in later life with a pigeon on her shoulder.

Violet (known as C.V.) was Economics tutor at St Anne's College (formerly the Society of Home Students and then St Anne's Society) from 1914 to 1945. She was a pioneer in Social Work training and did much voluntary work in Oxford, especially in the community. She was instrumental in starting the Rose Hill Community Centre. At her funeral, Lord Redcliffe-Maud described her as a saint. (See Wartime section).

Her sister, Ruth Butler, was assistant to the first Principal of St Anne's, Bertha Johnson, and later modern history tutor and Vice-Principal until 1942. (All Butler photographs courtesy Christina Colvin.)

The Cairns Family

Sir Hugh Cairns (1896–1952) was the first Nuffield Professor of Surgery at the University of Oxford. Hugh, son of an Australian village carpenter, first came to Oxford as a Rhodes Scholar to Balliol. He won a rowing blue and was one of the brilliant young men who married a daughter of A.L. Smith (see Smith Family), the Master of Balliol. He became Britain's foremost brain surgeon and his early death was a great loss to the country.

Barbara Forster Smith, the youngest of the daughters of A.L. Smith, was at Girton College, Cambridge where, in 1917, she obtained honours in modern history (degrees not at that time being awarded to women). She was a strikingly beautiful woman; she and her sisters had been described as a 'bunch of roses scattered across the Broad'. Her mother liked Cairns from the start and liked to talk medicine with him. When Hugh went to ask A.L. Smith for the hand of his daughter, Mrs Smith intercepted him and told him not to worry her husband, saying that she did not usually bother him about even really important things such as that the cook is leaving. Hugh did not

have to do more and Barbara married him in November, 1921, the day after Hugh passed his exam for the Fellowship of the Royal College of Surgeons. They could not afford a honeymoon.

Hugh and Barbara Cairns in 1947.

The Cairns children at Christmas, 1937. Left to right: Liz, Margaret, David and John in the garden of their home, 29 Charlbury Road. They had just moved in and were wearing sandals or light shoes in the snow because they had left their boots behind. The first owner of the house was Ernest William Ainley-Walker (1871–1955), Reader in Pathology, who took a major part in the design of the house. It was built in 1915.

At one time there were four Professors living within a stone's throw of each other at the corner of Charlbury and Belbroughton Roads. (Photographs courtesy Mrs Liz Nussbaum).

The Chaudhuris

Nirad Chaudhuri, the author and broadcaster, was born in Bengal on 23 November 1897 and is therefore one of North Oxford's distinguished centenarians. He was awarded an Honorary C.B.E. in 1992.

Mr Chaudhuri made his name by writing *The Autobiography of an Unknown Indian* (1951) and has written many successful books since. Educated at Calcutta University, he has been resident in the U.K. since 1970, most of that time in Oxford. He has lived in Lathbury Road since 1982. Valentine Cunningham, author of a chapter in Volume VIII of *The History of the University of Oxford,* describes Chaudhuri as the 'most famous Indian writer resident outside India.'

The Chaudhuris married in 1932 and have three sons. They had a very happy marriage — she died in 1994 — neither encountering any prejudice and often being invited out to dinner. He and his wife shared an interest in birds and music and, because she could distinguish the songs of British birds, and he could not she had recordings made for him of, for example, thrushes and nightingales. He loves all European music but does play Bengali songs to get into a 'writing mood.'

Nirad Chaudhuri at Lathbury Road five months before his hundredth birthday (July 1997). 'Nothing is certain but death', he says. From the age of 16 he always knew death could come at any moment and believes one should be able to shed every desire. He is a well-known figure in his local shopping centre where he goes on foot and is noted for his dapper attire.

Outside the front door of his home in July 1997.

The Davis Family

Henry William Carless Davis, C.B.E. (1874–1928) was Regius Professor of modern history at Oxford and a Fellow of Oriel College. He was an outstanding and influential teacher. He and his wife Jennie (who usually called herself Mrs Carless Davis) had three sons. Patrick became a solicitor and Godfrey and Ralph both historians (the latter Professor of medieval history at Birmingham University). H.W.C. Davis edited *The Dictionary of National Biography* from 1919 to 1928. They lived in Park Town. Jessie was a widow for 28 years and died in 1969.

Professor H.W.C. Davis with his three sons in about 1920. Left to right: Ralph, Patrick and Godfrey.

Jennie Carless Davis with her three sons taken in 1933 in the garden of their Park Town home. Left to right: Patrick, Godfrey and Ralph. (Photographs courtesy of Mrs Eleanor Davis.)

The Drivers

The Driver family in their garden at Christ Church in about 1904 (courtesy of Miss Mary Driver). Left to right: Godfrey (1892–1975), later Sir Godfrey, who when married first lived in St Giles, then (from 1930) at 14 Charlbury Road and finally (from 1953) at 41 Park Town. Cyril Driver, Dr S.R.Driver (1846–1914), Regius Professor of Hebrew and Canon of

Christ Church, who lived with his family in a house in Tom Quad, Sylvia, who later married Colonel Ralph Symonds and lived for many years at 4 Linton Road, Mabel Driver (wife of S.R.) née Burr, Cynthia, who before her marriage lived with her mother at 107 Banbury Road and ran a small school for pre-preparatory children. Sir Godfrey followed in his father's footsteps and also became Regius Professor of Hebrew at Oxford. In the First World War he had won the M.C.

The Foster-Carters

After the wedding of Aylmer Foster-Carter, taken in the back garden of St Andrew's Vicarage, Linton Road in 1947. (Courtesy Miss Lois Foster-Carter). The Reverend George Foster-Carter was a well-loved Vicar of St Andrew's Church, Linton Road from 1939 to 1954. There was still clothes rationing in 1947 but Lois Foster-Carter had just come

out of the ATS (the women's section of the Army) and her new sister-in-law was able to use her 'de-mob' clothing coupons for her trousseau. Back row, left to right: The Rev. George Foster-Carter, Lois Foster-Carter, the best man, Aylmer Foster-Carter (son of George) and his bride Ethna, the Bishop of Rochester, Christopher Chavasse (former Master of St Peter's Hall), uncle of the groom, Pamela Foster-Carter, Mr Price-Thomas (chest consultant) who gave away the bride. Front row: Felicity Foster-Carter, Miss Maureen McDermot, the bride's sister.

The Galbraiths

The Galbraiths bought their house, 1 Garford Road, off the drawing board in about 1928 when Blackhall Farm sold off some land for a small development of houses.

The future Mrs Ena Galbraith at Lady Margaret Hall in her hockey uniform in about 1917. She captained the team.

Both Professor Vivian Hunter Galbraith and his wife Ena were mediaevalists. After Lady Margaret Hall, she took a PhD at Manchester University and taught at Oxford. In the Second World War she joined the WRENS (the Women's Naval Service) at Portsmouth. He was made a Fellow of Balliol in 1928. In 1948 he became Regius Professor of History at Oxford. They had three children, Jane, Jim and Mary. The latter became Principal of St Hilda's College.

Jim, Jane and baby Mary in the garden of 1 Garford Road.

Jim and Mary Galbraith with their nurse, Nurse Pridham, in the early 1930s. Trained Norland nannies were employed by those families who could afford them but when money was tight they were replaced by country girls, such as Phyllis (by the Galbraiths) and Winnie (by the Spokes family). It was these girls' strict morals which sometimes influenced the children than the families themselves.

Although the Garford Road house was comparatively small, the Galbraiths, nevertheless, even in the beginning when he was on the salary of a very junior don, employed domestic staff. Shown here in 1936 in front of their house are, left to right: Mr Trollope, the gardener, Herring, the cook-general (see Visiting), Phyllis, the nanny, Mary Galbraith and Chris, the dog. (Photographs courtesy of Mrs Mary Moore.)

The Garnetts

The Maxwell Garnetts lived at 37 Park Town from 1939 to 1955 when they moved to the Isle of Wight. James Clerk Maxwell Garnett, C.B.E. (1880–1958) was an educationist and Secretary of the League of Nations Union. His wife Margaret was the daughter of Sir Edward Poulton (see Families) and they had six children.

Above: Maxwell and Margaret (née Poulton) Garnett in November 1921 with their four eldest children. Left to right: Michael (3), Pauline (5), Peggy (9) and John (4 months). (Courtsey of Mrs Peggy Jay.)

Right: the Garnett children with their father in 1924. Back row, left to right: Pauline (Mrs Roland Hunt), Peggy (Mrs Douglas Jay). Centre: Michael, Maxwell, John. Front: Priscilla (the baby) (Mrs Claude Lyle).

Maxwell and Margaret Garnett with five of their six children in August 1956. Left to right: Nicolas (the youngest), Priscilla, John, Michael and Pauline. Peggy is out of the picture. (Courtsey of Mrs Peggy Jay.)

No. 37 Park Town taken in 1997. During the Second World War the garage, seen here, was the home of a community kitchen for the whole of Park Town, set up on the initiative of Margaret Garnett. It was mainly due to the persuasive powers of Maxwell Garnett that residents of Park Town gave up their iron railings in order to help the war effort. His wife, however, would not allow the removal of the railings at the back of the house or those on either side of their front door steps.

The Gilletts

Arthur and Margaret Gillett (née Clark) were contemporaries at Cambridge and both belonged to the Society of Friends. He was a partner in Gillett's Bank at Oxford. They married in 1909 and lived at 102 Banbury Road. She was a granddaughter of John Bright and a close friend of General Jan Smuts (later Prime Minister of the Union of South Africa).

In 1909, Smuts came to England on a delegation and twice stayed with the Gilletts in Oxford. Arthur remembered the General walking up and down the garden exclaiming 'What a world it is,' meaning that the world was a happy and glorious place. Margaret had cause to chide Smuts when he became such a good friend of Arthur's that his letters were addressed to him and not to her. Nevertheless, in 1911 when their first son was born they called him Jan. During the First World War, Smuts was a member of the War Cabinet, staying in London but visiting other places at weekends.

In 1917 Smuts spent more than a dozen weekends with the Gilletts and went with them to the Downs in Summer. Their quiet Quaker household in North Oxford became a second home which he preferred to others, despite well-known acquaintances who had pressed him to stay with them such as the Archbishop of Canterbury, the Duchess of Rutland, Lady Astor (at Cliveden) and Mrs Asquith who pursued him with 'a fierce possessive ardour.' The photograph (taken at 102 Banbury Road in 1917) shows on the back row, left to right: General Jan C. Smuts, John B. Clark, Margaret Gillett (née Clark). Front row: Nicholas (Nico), W.S. Clark, Jan Gillett, Alice Clark with Fara the dog.

In 1918 Smuts would come down to Oxford on a Friday night, play with the children next morning and then set off for a country outing with the Gilletts. He felt at rest with them and as his biographer, W.K. Hancock, said: they 'provided an outlet for his inner need to express himself without fear of being quoted or argued with . . . or made responsible in any way.'

The Gilis

Joan (John spelled the Catalan way) Gili came to England to live in 1934. First in London, having come from Barcelona (where his father had been in publishing), he ran the Dolphin bookshop and the Dolphin Book Company. He met his wife Elizabeth (née McPherson), then studying at University College, London (and later awarded a Henry fellowship at Yale University) almost on the day of his arrival as he was staying with her cousin; they married in June 1938.

In 1940 the Gilis moved to Park Town where for nearly three years they lived in a tiny one-room artist's studio. Although Oxford gave them a most friendly welcome, it had not been easy to find accommodation in wartime as there was prejudice against 'foreigners'. Park Town, however, was different as it was home to so many refugees.

In the studio, with its one northern window in the roof, they were unable to see out and had no running water and too little heat to warm the 20-foot high-ceilinged room. They made partitions of double bookshelves and, when a hip bath was brought out and filled from kettles, the dining-room table had to be moved. Elizabeth worked in Balliol with the Foreign Office research deparment while Joan carried on his book publishing and translating.

In April 1943 their son Jonathan was born. A police car came (substitute for an ambulance during the war) and took Elizabeth to the hospital for the birth. Joan, as a foreigner, was forbidden to go out after midnight and it was already late in the evening. Fortunately, the policeman took pity on them and allowed Joan to accompany Elizabeth. Despite these restrictions on his movements Joan headed up the Park Town firewatchers.

Life was not easy in the studio. When the weather was fine the little boy's playpen was placed on the pavement outside and people came to talk to him. In winter the house was exceedingly cold. Once Jonathan wanted to bring back some snowballs from the Parks and his mother warned him that they would melt. However, they did not and were exactly the same size next morning.

No. 14 Fyfield Road from the garden, once known as Norham Lodge. One day in 1945 the Gilis heard that the house (owned by Mrs Schiele who had married an Argentinian) was for sale. She was sorry for their little boy who lived in a place where he could not see out and gave them precedence. The Gilis paid £2,500 for the 25 years remaining of the lease. They moved to Cumnor in 1969.

The Gilis at 14 Fyfield Road in about 1949 with their three children. Left to right: Martin Lluis Gili, Jonathan Francesc Gili and Katherine (Katy) Montserrat Gili. (Photographs courtesy Joan and Elizabeth Gili.)

The Haldanes

Professor John Scott Haldane, CH, FRS, MD (1860–1936) and his wife Louisa Kathleen Haldane (née Trotter) (1863–1961) lived at 'Cherwell' at the bottom of Linton Road. Earlier they had lived at 11 Crick Road. They arranged a 100-year lease from St John's College on 11 acres of land and the house was built by George Gardiner; they did not employ an architect. Gardiner was also responsible for 16–20 Linton Road. He was known to have no doubts about his own qualifications although he made mistakes with the electric wiring. When the family moved in, the furniture from Scotland was conveyed in three railway vans and the road leading to the house, being but a farm track, was broken up by the furniture vans.

'Cherwell' in 1914. It was built in about 1910 and was demolished when Wolfson College was erected on the site. There was a spectacular view of the river across the meadows which were full of wild flowers. The Haldanes generously invited the local children to fish off their dock at the water's edge. The house was decorated with busts of Disraeli and (later) of Chamberlain. Despite the fact that the house had ten bedrooms there was only one bath, a gigantic iron one. The only running water was in the housemaid's sink and had to be carried upstairs in bowls. The Haldane arms, together with the motto 'Suffer' were over the door. One of their grandchildren misread it as 'Supper'.

J.S. Haldane in 1928 after receiving his Companion of Honour. He was a Fellow of New College and a physiologist and philosopher. He did important work on respiration, especially at high altitudes, the ventilation of mines, factories and submarines, diving apparatus and, in 1915, gas masks. His granddaughter, Mrs Lois Godfrey, remembers that he always wore a gold chain across his chest, stretching from pocket to pocket. In one pocket was his watch and in the other a gold case in which he kept chocolate for small children. To reach it they had to climb up above the overhang of his stomach. He always smelled of Bunsen burners and chemicals. He had about five laboratories and a gas chamber for his experiments at 'Cherwell'. After his death they became apple stores. His dying words were: 'I've just been having a most interesting conversation with Dr. Priestley' (the discoverer of oxygen).

Louisa Haldane, J.R.'s wife, was very pro-Empire and supported the Victoria League. She made lists of Empire goods which wives of dons should seek out at Elliston's and Grimbly Hughes and sent out her son and daughter to enrol village children in the League of Empire. She received the OBE for her work among Colonial students.

Plays were performed in the garden of 'Cherwell'. The young Haldanes, John Burdon Sanderson (JBS), the geneticist, and Naomi (born 1897) later Naomi Mitchison, the author, took part. Naomi often wrote the words and one play, *The Prisoner of War*, which she wrote in 1914, organised by Mrs Haldane on behalf of the Child Emigration Society, was described by a reviewer as 'one of the cleverest amateur entertainments . . . ever given in Oxford' and 'remarkable for one so young.' This is the cast of Gilbert Murray's translation of Aristophones' *The Frogs* performed at 'Cherwell'. In the centre is Naomi Haldane and in furs is her brother Jack (J.B.S.). On his right is G.R. Mitchison. Seated, far right, is Lewis Gielgud, brother of John, who wrote plays. Far right, standing, is Miss Blockie, the Haldane's governess.

The cast of one of the plays performed at 'Cherwell' in 1914, taken at New College after the performance. Third row: 6th from left G.R. Mitchison, 7th from left Lewis Gielgud, 8th from left Mrs Haldane. Behind Mrs. Haldane in the back row is Aldous Huxley. Second row: 5th from left Miss Blockie (governess), 6th from left Naomi Haldane, 7th from left J.B.S (Jack) Haldane. (All Haldane photographs courtesy of Mrs Lois Godfrey.)

The Maclagans

Michael and Jean (née Garnett) Maclagan live at 20 Northmoor Road, the former home of the Tolkien family (see further on in this chapter). The first resident there was Basil Blackwell, the well-known publisher and bookseller. The architect was F.E. Oppenheimer (1926).

No. 20 Northmoor Road in 1997.

Michael Maclagan, CVO, FSA, Richmond Herald of Arms, Emeritus Fellow of Trinity College, Oxford, rose to the rank of Major in the Second World War and was Mayor of Oxford in 1970–71. J.R.R. Tolkien wrote his books at a desk which was situated in the corner of this room on the left. (Photograph taken in 1991.)

Ianthe Maclagan's fifth birthday party, July 1957, in the garden of 20 Northmoor Road with neighbours and their children. Back row, left to right: Marcia Gray with Charlotte, Gill Williams with Janet, Aunt Dora Maclagan, Janet (later Baroness) Young with Alix. Front row: Jean Maclagan with Ianthe and Helen (looking away) behind, Susan Paget, Caroline Silver, Michael Maclagan (with gramophone), Claire Barnett.

Michael and Jean Maclagan, who married in 1949, with members of their family on the occasion of Michael's 80th birthday party. (Photographs courtesy of Michael and Jean Maclagan.)

The Max Müllers

When Frederick Max Müller (1823–1900) first came to Oxford in 1848, what impressed him most, as he recalled in his autobiography, 'even more than the hospitality of Oxford, was the real friendship shown to an unkown German scholar. I must have seemed a very strange bird, such as had never before built his nest in Oxford.' It never entered his wildest dreams that in a few years time he would be a Fellow 'of the most exclusive of colleges' (Christ Church) and a married one at that (not even invented then) and the first Professor of Philology. In fact, Max Müller, described as the greatest Sanskrit scholar of all time, had more honours to come, including a fellowship of All Souls and membership of the Privy Council and therefore able to take the title of Right Honourable. In 1873, for instance, he dined with Prince Leopold (presumably when he was living at Wykeham House in the Banbury Road) who said that the Queen had charged him to tell Max Müller how pleased she was that he had decided to stay in England. He became a naturalised Englishman. Mrs Max Müller, who was British, was closely associated with the setting up of the women's colleges in Oxford.

No. 7 Norham Gardens ('Parks End'), originally the home of Professor Goldwin Smith which he had had built for himself on the edge of the Parks in 1862 as a bachelor's house. The nearest houses to the north at that time were in Park Town. The Max Müllers bought it at auction in 1867. Oliver Wendell Holmes, the poet, describing his visit to the Müllers in 1886, wrote:

> 'It was a lovely family picture, a pretty house, surrounded by attractive scenery, scholarship, refinement, simple elegance, giving distinction to a house which seemed a pattern of all we could wish to see beneath an English roof.'

Other well-known visitors were the Rt Hon W.E. Gladstone, the poet Emerson and Prince Leopold.

Max Müller at the age of 40 and in later life in the library at 7 Norham Gardens. He had 13,000 volumes here. Following his funeral in St. Mary's in the High Street in 1900, nearly all the large congregation walked on foot to Holywell Cemetery (St Cross) where he is buried. His grave there is still much visited nearly a century later.

The Murrays

What was described as the greatest dictionary of modern times, *The Oxford English Dictionary,* was edited by James Murray (1837–1915) in the garden of his home, 78 Banbury Road, called 'Sunnyside', after his former Mill Hill home. Having moved to Oxford in 1885, he built what was called the 'Scriptorium' where the work was done with the aid of assistants. It had to be sunk three feet into the ground, and was damp and cold as a consequence, to suit Professor Dicey who lived next door and did not want to see it over the wall. Murray did this under protest, regretting that 'no trace of such a place of real work should be seen by fastidious and otiose Oxford'.

'Sunnyside'. the home of the Murrays, built in 1882 (Wilkinson and Moore), as it was in about 1887. The Sciptorium (or 'The Scrippy' as the children called it) is on the right.

Sir James Murray (knighted in 1908) in the Scriptorium. He was largely self-educated and came from a humble home in a small Scottish village. He thought his task of editing would take 10 years but it had not been completed on his death 35 years later. Oxford gave him an Hon. LLD in 1914. He realised that once he had moved to Oxford he was bound to the dictionary for the rest of his working life.

Murray had another claim to fame because he was a friend of Alexander Graham Bell and taught him about electricty. Bell, in return, gave him the very first telephone (patented in January 1877) as a memento and called Murray 'the grandfather of the telephone'.

The Scriptorium no longer exists but this plaque (courtesy of the present owner) commemorates its existence in the garden of 78 Banbury Road.

SCRIPTORIUM
ON THIS SITE
SIR JAMES MURRAY
COMPILED THE OXFORD ENGLISH
DICTIONARY FROM
1885 - 1915

The Murrays in about 1892. James was known as 'the Dic' and his family the 'little Dics'. James and Ada Murray had 11 children who were given names from Anglo-Saxon literature. Jowett was, however, named after the great Benjamin Jowett, Vice-Chancellor of the University, who was a close friend. The children were given pocket money for helping to sort the dictionary slips. Murray was always in financial difficulty, having to pay back the loan on the house and not receiving much in salary. Ada Murray had sought information on family planning before she came to Oxford but the primitive advice given to her by a doctor was to 'slide down the banisters'. She learnt better when she came to Oxford but still had five more children. He worried about how he was going to educate them all. Back row, left to right: Wilfred, Hilda, Oswyn, Ethelwyn. Middle row: Elsie, Harold, James, Ada, Ethelbert, Aelfric. Front row: Rosfrith, Gwyneth, Jowett. (Family photographs courtesy of K.M. Elizabeth Murray, author of *Caught in the Web of Words, James Murray and the Oxford English Dictionary* published by Yale University Press.)

The Oslers

In 1905, the Oslers came to North Oxford when William Osler (1849–1919) was appointed Regius Professor of Medicine at the University. They left behind their home in a noisy corner of Baltimore, Maryland where he had been Professor of Medicine at Johns Hopkins University. Osler was the best-known physician of his time and was a great teacher. One of his charms was the interest he took in obscure workers in any field of medicine. He was Canadian, born in the backwoods of Ontario, seventh in a missionary's family. He was made a baronet in 1911.

William Osler in about 1909.

Grace Osler was American, the daughter of John and Susan Revere of Boston, and widow of one of Osler's best friends, Dr S.D. Gross, who had been regarded as the 'dean of American surgery'. She was about 38 when she wed Osler, then 52, and someone warned her that she was going to marry a man who had books all over the floor.

They stayed first at 7 Norham Gardens, which Mrs Max Müller (then widowed) let them have furnished. Mrs Osler wrote to her mother: '. . . nothing could be more wonderful than the lilacs, laburnum and hawthorn. It is one huge mass — up and down every street and in every garden, hanging from the roofs'. Mrs Max Müller had given them a wonderful welcome with a butler at the door and maids in the hall.

After much searching they found 13 Norham Gardens, getting possession of it in August 1906. However, because they wanted alterations they did not move in until January 1907.

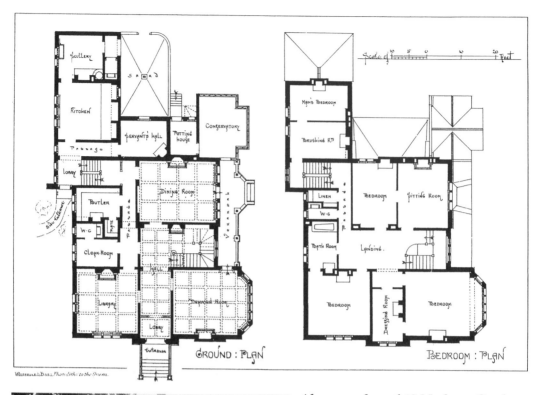

GROUND : PLAN

BEDROOM : PLAN

Above: a plan of 13 Norham Gardens from the architect, Wilkinson's book. Note the bathroom on the bedroom floor. Mrs Osler amazed Oxford plumbers when as the wife of the Regius Profesor of Medicine, and inspecting a porcelain bath, while backs were turned, she climbed into to it to see if it was long enough. When she ordered four of them they could not understand why the family and their guests needed so much washing.

Left: the front door of 13 Norham Gardens (1997). Sir William Osler gave serious dinner parties for his students. After the meal the butler would bring in a trayful of books and Osler expected them to talk about these over the port as part of their medical training.

No. 13 Norham Gardens from the garden (south) side (1997). Between 1938 and 1952 it housed Home Students (later St Anne's College). Miss Fairbairn (nicknamed 'Fairy') was the popular hostess. During the 1939—40 war a nursery school for evacuee children was held in what was once the Osler's dining room.

The Oslers had one child, Revere, who was the great-great grandson of the famous American Paul Revere. There was an unusual companionship between Osler and his son. Tragically, Revere was killed in Flanders in the 1914—18 War and this broke Sir William's heart.

The Poultons

George Palmer (of Huntley and Palmer's biscuits and MP for Reading), bought the lease of Wykeham House, 56 Banbury Road, in 1881 for his daughter Emily and her husband Edward Bagnall Poulton. He had doubts about Emily marrying an impecunious don and there had been some delay before he agreed to the wedding. He need not have worried because E.B. (1856—1943) became Hope Professor of Zoology in 1893 and was knighted in 1935. People remarked that he 'married the biscuit and got the tin'.

Wykeham House (right), home of the Poultons from 1881. (Taken by P.S. Spokes in 1965). Norham House, No. 58, designed by the same architect, John Gibbs, is on the left.

Pevsner described Wykeham House as a 'yellow-brick nightmare castle' and even Ruskin thought it hideous. On the front of the house, helping to make the chimney more interesting, is a statue of William of Wykeham, the founder of New College, by W. Forsyth of Worcester. The house, the origin of whose associaton with New College's founder is uncertain, was built for Henry Hatch in 1865—66. Hatch ran a drapery store in Magdalen Street and he opened the Victoria Theatre behind his shop. He never lived at No. 56 but let it to various people including Prince Leopold, Queen Victoria's younger son, who lived there while he was an undergraduate at Christ Church. It was to Wykeham House that Ruskin came to teach the Prince to draw. Poulton made two extensions to the house to accommodate his growing family. In 1904, on the occasion of the 21st birthday of Teddy (Edward) Poulton, they had nearly 100 guests to a party in the playroom at the top of the house.

Wykeham House in 1994 soon after the new extension was built by the present occupiers, the University Careers Service (formerly known as the Appointments Committee.)

Edward Bagnall Poulton and his wife Emily, member of the Council of Somerville College (1884–1939) with their five children: Janet (on her father's knee), Margaret (left) and Hilda and (in front) Edward (left) and Ronald, taken in 1895. By 1919 all but Margaret and Edward had died.

Janet Poulton (later wife of Dr. Charles Symonds) in the garden of Wykeham House in about 1902. She died in a bicycle accident in 1919 at the age of 26 when her son Ronald was three and son Richard nine months. In 1903, when Janet was eleven, the Duchess of Albany, widow of Prince Leopold (who had died in 1884), and her daughter Princess Alice, came to tea and looked over the house where Prince Leopold had lived.

Margaret Poulton (Mrs Maxwell Garnett) and Hilda (Mrs Ainley-Walker), who died in 1917, painted in about 1907 by Thomas Cooper Gotch. During the Second World War, when Wykeham House was a nurses' home, the boy friends of the nurses threw darts at this picture. It was restored in the 1980s.

Janet Poulton with her brother Ronald in about 1912. Ronald played Rugby football for England and his record of tries in one game while playing for Oxford University has never been surpassed. He was killed in the First World War in May 1915. It was said of him after his death: 'One would never have guessed in talking to him that he was the idol of the whole youth of Britain'. He had been chosen as Palmer heir and took the name Poulton-Palmer.

Ronald Poulton-Palmer from a contemporary cartoon. He captained Oxford and also, in 1914, the England grand slam team. It is said that his legendary rugger swerve came from playing hide and seek in the Isle of Wight. He shared a memorial service with Rupert Brooke at Rugby School.

Sir Edward Poulton, FRS and Lady Poulton with their two surviving children and grand-children in 1928. Back row, left to right: Ronald Symonds, Pauline (Mrs Roland Hunt), Peggy (née Garnett, Mrs Douglas Jay), Edward Maclean Poulton, Richard Symonds. Middle row: Christopher Poulton, Margaret Poulton (née Garnett), Sir Edward with Penelope Poulton on his lap, Emily, Lady Poulton, with Priscilla Garnett on her lap, Edward Palmer-Poulton, Ronald Poulton. Front row: John Garnett, Janet Poulton, Michael Poulton. (See also Garnetts,)

The Simons

After Hitler was appointed Chancellor of Germany in January 1933, the first measures were taken against Jews and those of Jewish parentage. Franz Simon was not a practising Jew but in Breslau, where he was Professor of physical chemistry, he had to hand in his passport. When he flung it down he asked the official whether he wanted his Iron Cross as well. He had earned this in the First World War. Simon was one of the first to realise that there was no future for Jewish people in Germany. Even when Jewish academics were dismissed after a lifetime's service and some even driven to suicide, Simon's friends could not understand why he wanted to leave Germany.

In August 1922, Franz married Charlotte Munchhausen who came from a wealthy Jewish family. Their dining-room, for instance, was capable of seating 60 people. Severe inflation meant that most of Simon's money had little value. In 1931, Simon had been appointed a visiting professor in California and even then he was so worried about the situation in Germany that he arranged for Charlotte and their two children, Kay and Dorothy, to reside in Switzerland while he was away.

Franz (later Sir Francis) Simon leaving Breslau railway station in 1933 en route for Oxford. Having already made a name for himself — he was the first person to liquefy helium in the United States — he was invited by F.A. Lindemann (later Lord Cherwell), Dr Lee's Professor of Experimental Philosophy at Oxford, to come to work in the Clarendon Laboratory. Together with Gilbert Murray and his wife Lady Mary Murray, Lindemann had persuaded ICI to finance fellowships for German scientists. Negotiations were conducted in code, Simon being known as 'high pressure composer' and Nicholas Kurti (later Professor and CBE) who also came from Breslau, was 'low pressure composer.'

Charlotte (later Lady) Simon with her daughters Kay and Dorothy in the garden of 10 Belbroughton Road in 1934. The Simons enjoyed Oxford where they were given a hospitable welcome and made many friends. Charlotte said that she would never return to Germany even if it meant scrubbing floors all her life. Their home became a haven for refugees but they had sleepless nights worrying about those who could not find jobs and who had to return to Germany to a gruesome fate.

Sir Francis Simon relaxing in Oxford in 1953. He became a British subject in 1938 and was awarded the CBE in the first New Year's honours after the Second World War. He was amused to think that he was the only holder of a British CBE and the German Iron Cross. He was knighted in 1954 in recognition of his great scientific achievements and public service. Sadly, he died in October 1956, less than a month after he had been appointed to succeed Lord Cherwell as Dr Lee's Professor and head of the Clarendon Laboratory. (All the above photographs courtesy of Lady Simon.)

Lady Simon in 1997 seated on one of the pieces of furniture which came from Germany. Now a centenarian, she clearly remembers her first few months in Oxford 64 years ago. House-hunting, she had specified central heating and was surprised when the estate agent remarked: 'But have you *seen* Oxford houses?'. Her husband had an impish sense of humour and a rather happy-go-lucky attitude to money. Charlotte's efforts to economise he called 'a Woolworth's mentality'. However, he accepted the fact that they could not afford the £1,000 needed to put in central heating. As he did not approve of gas fires they suffered much from the cold for many years.

The Slaters

Left to right: Dr Gilbert Slater, his wife Violet Slater (née Oakeshott), Eliot Slater, their son (at back), Leonid Pasternak, his wife Rosalia (née Koffman), Eliot's parents-in-law, at 20 Park Town which they had bought in 1912. Gilbert and Violet had three sons, Owen, the eldest, Eliot and Patrick.

Owen Slater and his wife Nando came to live at 12 Bradmore Road in 1932. The first owner of the lease had been John Galpin, the auctioneer. Owen was a maths teacher at Southfield School which later became Oxford School. He was a knowledgeable bee-keeper. Nando was a hostess for the Society of Home Students (later St Anne's College). They housed the first married woman undergraduate, only allowed then because the couple, Americans Rudolf and Ann Light, had married before they came to Oxford. The Owen Slaters had three children, Martin, Margaret and Eithne. Margaret Slater (Mrs Bonfiglioli) — see 18 Norham Gardens — remembers in the late 1940s the St Anne's girls being worried about what would happen if they acquired a first-class degree and their fiancés got a second. Would the engagement be broken off?

Eliot married Lydia Pasternak and her parents, Leonid and Rosalia, came to live at 20 Park Town in the late 1930s. They had moved to Germany from Russia in the 1920s. Leonid was well-known as a Russian impressionist painter and was a friend of Tolstoy and illustrated his books. Rosalia was a concert pianist. Their eldest son was the poet and novelist Boris Pasternak. Eliot and Lydia (née Pasternak) had four children, Michael, Nicolas, Catherine (Dr Oppenheimer) and Ann (Dr Pasternak Slater), who is a Fellow of St. Anne's College. Ann is married to the poet Craig Raine who is a Fellow of New College. They have one daughter and three sons and still live at 20 Park Town.

Michael and Nicolas Slater with their Nanny in the Second World War at 20 Park Town. Note the wartime sandbags. (Photographs courtesy of Dr Ann Pasternak Slater.)

The A.L. Smiths

Lionel Smith and his wife Mary had nine children and were the founders of a dynasty which had a great influence on Oxford life. They married in 1879 and lived first (until 1893) at 'Somerley', 7 Crick Road, which Mrs A.L. Smith described as 'ugly and inconvenient' with a garden of 'mostly brickbats and stones'. They had been advised against a smaller home in Canterbury Road as there would not have been room for a nursery.

The Smiths were always having to put up students of Lionel's, who was a don at Balliol College, and looking back (in her *Life of A.L. Smith,* 1928),

'Somerley' (taken in 1997).

Mary Smith wondered how they managed to 'put up three men as well as our own nursery party and three maids, but our houses always had a strange elasticity. True', she wrote, 'the children had but one room for night and day nursery and I always had at least one with me.' She once made a 'skimpy little frock' for one of the babies out of the black velvet sleeves of the proctor's gown which her husband wore during his year of office — 'a most illegal proceeding, I believe.'

Six of their nine children were born in Crick Road. Even when she was pregnant Mrs Smith had to have a couple of pupils living there too to be coached and tutored by her husband. Jowett (Master of Balliol) had requested and Jowett could never be refused. In 1893, they moved to 'King's Mound' which had been built as a Balliol tutor's house on the site of the Civil War fortifications in Mansfield Road.

A.L. Smith (1850–1924) in 1923. He helped to build up the history school at Oxford. He was Modern History tutor at Balliol in 1879, Fellow in 1882, Dean in 1907 and Master in 1916.

Mrs A.L. Smith, described as a 'great Victorian lady', with seven of her nine children in 1895. She had two sons and seven daughters. Lionel, born 1880, was the eldest. The youngest, Hubert, was born in 1899. All seven girls married. Carola Oman in *An Oxford Childhood,* (1976) wrote: 'There were seven Misses Smith . . . and one of them married happily nearly every year. They had a very high standard of placid, blonde good looks and intelligence.' Gertrude wed Harold Hartley, later Brigadier General Sir Harold, a science tutor at Balliol and President of the British Association. Molly married Frederick Barrington-Ward who was a KC, Metropolitan Magistrate, a Recorder and Fellow of All Souls. He died in 1937 and Molly later married Sir Frederick Hamilton. A Cambridge man, he went to South Africa and was Editor of *The Johannesburg Star.* He was sent from there to Cecil Rhodes in an attempt to stop the Jameson Raid. Dorothy married Robert (Robin) Hodgkin, lecturer in Modern History and later Provost of the Queens' College, Oxford.

Miriam (Biddy) married Reader (later Sir Reader) Bullard KCMG KCB, the diplomat, lecturer and writer. He was Ambassador to Persia and Director of the Oxford Institute of Commonwealth Studies. Lady Bullard is shown here with her four children in Crick Road where they lived from 1931 to 1946. Left to right: Dorothea, Giles, Lady Bullard, Julian and Godfrey. The photograph was taken in 1943. Note the painted curbs to enable people to see the edges of the roads in the wartime black-out. (Courtesy of Sir Julian Bullard.)

The fifth daughter, Margaret's husband was John Gordon Jameson who was called to the Scottish bar and became a Sheriff. Rosalind wed first Edward Murray Wrong, a Canadian who was a lecturer in Colonial History at Oxford from 1919 to 1924. He died in 1928. Later, she married Sir Henry Clay, the economist and Warden of Nuffield College. Barbara, the youngest, became the wife of Hugh Cairns (see Families).

The Somersets

The Somerset family in the garden of their house, 120 Banbury Road, which is on the southern corner of Belbroughton Road. Both photographs were taken in the 1930s. The house looks much the same today.

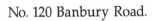

No. 120 Banbury Road.

William Somerset was Assistant Librarian at the Bodleian Library from 1905 until 1945. Ruby Somerset was Tutor in English Language at Somerville and St Hugh's Colleges. After she married in 1921 she continued teaching from home on a part-time basis. She was always in demand and later one of her pupils told her daughter that they would never have managed Anglo-Saxon at all without her excellent guidance. They are shown with their children, Helen (Mrs Henry Lock, who kindly lent the photographs) and Fitzroy.

The Spokes Family

The Spokes family in the summer of 1947 in the garden of their home, 26 Charlbury Road, which Peter and Lilla Spokes moved into in 1924 and which was their home until 1949. The family enjoyed dressing up as can be seen in this photograph. Lilla (née Clayton) and Peter came to 26 Charlbury Road soon after their marriage. There was a tradition that the most recent bride should wear her wedding dress out to dinner and be taken in on the arm of the host, however superior he was or however eminent the other women present. She remembered one of the first dinner parties they went to was at 'Cherwell' where she was taken in to dine on the arm of Professor Haldane. Back row, left to right: Peter Russell, John. Seated: Lilla, Rodney and Peter Spencer. Front: Mary and Ann. It is one of the few photographs of the whole family because Peter (evacuated with Ann to the USA in 1940) remained in America and became an American citizen. Rodney was born in 1943.

Spokes family group outside St Andrew's Church, Linton Road before the wedding of Penelope Bridges (next-door neighbour at No. 24 Charlbury Road) and Patrick Nairne, 18th September 1948. Left to right: Mary, Peter, John, Ann, Lilla and Rodney. Peter Spencer (1893–1976) was the first Secretary of the Imperial Forestry Institute in Oxford. Later he worked at the Bodleian Library and was a pioneer of the conservation of buildings. He served on the City Council and was Lord Mayor of Oxford in 1968. Lilla also became a City Councillor in later life.

The Stradlings

A. Louise Stradling with, left to right, daughters Rachel, Penelope and Mary outside 3 Charlbury Road in 1923. The owner has not been identified.

William Stradling (right) with G.C. Vassall. Both were popular masters at the Dragon School. The Stradlings lived at 3 Charlbury Road just across the way from the school.

Mary, Penelope and Rachel Stradling taken in 1938. Penelope served on Oxford City Council and chaired the Education Committee. She was married to Sir Harold Thompson, Professor of Chemistry at Oxford. He founded the Pegasus football club (the name being suggested by Penelope) and was Chairman of the Football Association from 1976 to 1981. The Thompsons lived in Linton Road for many years. (Photographs courtesy of Mrs A.R. Blaney.)

The Tolkiens

The Tolkiens came to live in North Oxford, at 22 Northmoor Road, in 1925 when J.R.R. (John Ronald Reuel) (1892–1978) was appointed Professor of Anglo-Saxon at the University. He had been much influenced by Joseph Wright, editor of *The English Dialect Dictionary* who had been Tolkien's boss at Leeds University. It was during time in hospital in the First World War that Tolkien began work on his first book, *The Silmarillion.* However, it was *The Hobbit,* which grew out of the stories told to his children, and *The Lord of the Rings* which achieved such acclaim and lasting fame. In 1945 he became Professor of English Language and Literature and was created CBE in 1972. Ronald (as he was known to the family) did not have rooms in college but bicycled into town on his high-seated bicycle. This meant he saw more of his children than dons who spent time in college.

A family tea party in the back garden of 22 Northmoor Road in May 1928. (Left to right: John Tolkien, Edith Tolkien, Michael Tolkien (back), J.R.R. Tolkien, Christopher Tolkien. The houses in the background are in Charlbury Road. The high brick walls are typical of those in North Oxford.

The Tolkiens at 20 Northmoor Road to which they moved from No. 22 in 1945. Standing, left to right: Michael (father of Michael George), Christopher (in Air Force uniform) and J.R.R. Tolkien. Seated: Michael George (J.R.R.'s grandson) on the lap of Joan Tolkien (daughter-in-law), Priscilla Tolkien, Mrs Edith Tolkien. (Photographs courtesy of Miss Priscilla Tolkien.)

The Parks and the River

There have been Parks in North Oxford since at least Stuart times. Charles II used to exercise his dogs there just as dogs take their owners there today. They were also known as Beaumont Fields and in earlier years Park was singular as well as plural. In 1853 the University purchased land from Merton College and from then onwards the planting of trees was planned. Before that it was just a grass field with a cart track across it from west to east approached from St Giles by a footpath between hedges where Keble Road is now. The Parks were laid out by James Bateman of Magdalen with a cricket ground, ornamental walks, a bathing place and a bridge over the Cherwell.

According to Mary Poynton, who lived in Fyfield Road in the 1920s, the size of the Parks can be reckoned by the fact that it took the park keeper (nowadays known as a Senior Technical Officer) an hour to go round locking all the gates at night. A croquet lawn, which many North Oxford people had in their own gardens, was also provided and is still played today. In 1887, for Queen Victoria's Jubilee, 7,000 children were entertained to tea in the Parks.

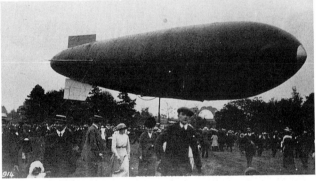

In 1913 an airship came down in the Parks and many North Oxford people, including James Murray, the lexicographer (see Families), rushed out early in the morning to see it. (Courtesy Jeremy's Postcards.)

A drawing of the round pond in the University Parks by Chiang Yee, in his book *The Silent Traveller in Oxford* (published by Methuen in 1944). He lived in North Oxford during the Second World War. This is how generations of children remember their well-loved pond.

The new pond, beside the Cherwell, 1997. It incorporates the old one which means that the pond is no longer round.

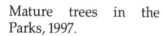

Mature trees in the Parks, 1997.

The Cricket Pavilion built in 1880. The architect was Sir Thomas Jackson. The cricket ground, made in 1881, is the only place in England where first-class cricket can be watched free of charge. Tennis has been played on the outfield of the cricket pitch for many years in the long vacations. (Photograph taken in 1997.)

Members of the Oxford University Croquet and Lawn Tennis Club in May 1995. Their grass courts are to the south-east of the cricket pitch. Left to right: Professor Derek Stacey, Dr David Stocker (Committee member), Bede Rundell (President) and Sir David Yardley (Committee member).

There is another well-known tennis club not far away in Benson Place to which some of the University Club also belong. Established in 1929, tennis has been played on the site of the Norham Gardens Lawn Tennis Club for a hundred years and it was about here that the first All-England Men's Doubles cup was contested before it moved to Wimbledon. It has six shale courts (formerly ten).

The brick-walled pathway into the Parks from Norham Gardens, the entrance most used by people living in Norham Manor, taken in 1997 looking towards the Parks. There are plans to move it southwards.

The river Cherwell runs along the eastern boundary of North Oxford and has always been a well-loved and well-used amenity. Here is a group on the banks of the river in the early 20th century.

The river and hump-back (rainbow) bridge drawn by Chiang-Yee and one of the illustrations in his book *The Silent Traveller in Oxford* (published by Methuen, 1944).

Punting, a popular pursuit, under the bridge in the Parks, early Spring 1996. The bridge was built in the 1920s.

Dragon school boys skating on the frozen Cherwell in 1940.

Cherwell Boathouse in the 1970s.

A landing stage between the Dragon school and the site of Wolfson College was established in 1901 by Tom Timms, the University Boat Club waterman. He hired out punts and skiffs on the Upper Cherwell. The boathouse, built in 1908/9 has his initials over the door and was called Timms' until about 1944. In 1946 the business was bought by Lt Commander Perowne, RN (Retd) and he established a restaurant there. It was sold in 1968 to Anthony Verdin, science graduate. He re-established the boat-building business and was at that time the only punt-builder in Oxford.

The river and the Cherwell boathouse in the summer of 1997 from Wolfson College bridge. The river provides a popular recreation for residents, undergraduates and students alike. LMH was one of the first to have a boathouse there and Wychwood girls have been taught to row on it since the early days of the school. In 1945/6, an undergraduate at St Hugh's college plucked up courage to ask the Principal, Miss Gwyer, why, when out with young men, they had to be off the river by 10 p.m. and the reply was: 'There are *creeks* you know, Miss W., there are *creeks.'*

Staff at the Cherwell boathouse with paddles and punt pole in the summer of 1997. Left to right: Roger Forster (the boss), Kenny Summers, Bob Dowling, Holly Forster, Alan ('Cotty') Cotmore.